This limited edition history of
This Far-off Sunset Land: A Pictorial History of Washington County, Oregon,
captures and preserves the stories, the memories, and the images
of Washington County and its communities.
Just as this publication is our salute to the beginning of a new millennium,
the Washington County Historical Society now
salutes and celebrates the generous public-spirited participation
of our financial backers:

Bretthauer Oil Company

Damerow Beaverton Ford

Adams, Hess, Moore & Co., Investment Consultants and Brokers

Prudential Northwest Properties

Reser's Fine Foods, Inc.

Pat Ritz, President, Oregon Title Insurance Co.

U.S. Bank

Proceeds from the sale of this volume will benefit

*You are a neighbor with those of the past as well as with those of the
present, if you walk where they have walked and live where they have lived.
YOU DO BELONG!*
–Charlotte McCartney, *Once Upon a Town,* 1985

THIS FAR-OFF SUNSET LAND

A Pictorial History of
Washington County, Oregon

by Carolyn M. Buan
With a Foreword by Jean M. Auel

I believe I have given about all the news at present and will close by requesting you all to write to a lonely wanderer away from home and kindred in this far off sunset land. . . .

—Jesse Moore, a pioneer of 1852
from a letter dated October 5, 1884
Greenville, Oregon, to his family in Fayetteville, Arkansas

THE
DONNING COMPANY
PUBLISHERS

For information, write:
The Donning Company/Publishers
184 Business Park Drive, Suite 106
Virginia Beach, VA 23462

Steve Mull, *General Manager*
Barbara A. Bolton, *Project Director*
Dawn V. Kofroth, *Assistant General Manager*
Richard A. Horwege, *Senior Editor*
Kevin M. Brown, *Art Director, Designer*
James Casper, *Imaging Artist*
Teri S. Arnold, *Senior Marketing Coordinator*

Library of Congress Cataloging-in-Publication Data

Buan, Carolyn M.
This far-off sunset land : a pictorial history of
Washington County, Oregon / by Carolyn M. Buan ;
with a foreword by Jean M. Auel.
p.   m.
Includes bibliographical references and index.
ISBN 1-57864-037-7 (hardcover : alk. paper)
1. Washington County (Or.)—History—Pictorial works.
2. Washington County (Or.)—Economic conditions—Pictorial
works. I. Title.
F882.W4B83   1999
979.5'43—dc21   98-26219
CIP

Printed in the United States of America

CONTENTS

FOREWORD

Histories of people and the places they inhabit have always been a subject of intense interest to many of us. It harks back to the basic questions of "Who are we?" and "Where did we come from?" It is probably why I have enjoyed learning and writing novels about the earliest appearance in Europe of modern humans, the ones we call Cro Magnons, who shared that cold, ancient, Ice Age land for ten thousand years with an earlier form of human, Neanderthals. The idea of two different kinds of humans—not just culturally, but physically different—living side by side in the same place is an appealing concept for a novelist.

But a similar circumstance occurred with the first European settlers in Oregon. Though perhaps not as radically different as Cro Magnons and Neanderthals, the cultural differences between the indigenous people, who knew the land intimately as hunters and gatherers as well as farmers, and the early-industrial-age European agriculturalists were perhaps as profound. But those indigenous people were once travelers from another place who subsequently settled here as well. People have

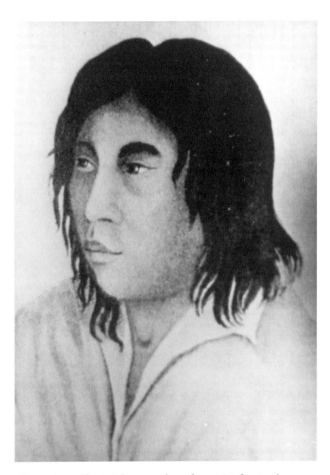

Drawing of a Kalapuya boy from Pickering's **The Races of Man**

always traveled and settled in different regions of this old planet; it is inherent in our nature.

Most Paleoanthropologists agree that the earliest beginnings of the animal we call human were in Africa. After a few million years the developing *Homo* species spread into the rest of what is called the Old World: Africa, Europe, Asia. It wasn't until the relatively recent times of the first early modern humans that Australia, and North and South America were populated; perhaps as long ago as forty or fifty thousand years ago for Australia, and maybe as recently as twelve to fourteen thousand for the Americas—though some evidence suggests that people arrived in the New World long before that.

The first people to inhabit our part of the planet came from the other side of the Pacific Ocean, from Asia. As the massive glaciers of the Ice Age trapped available water in miles-high pancakes of ice that spread out from the poles to cover over a fourth of earth's land, it lowered the level of the world's oceans by as much as three hundred feet. The coastlines probably extended beyond the continental shelf, and a strip of land a thousand miles wide was exposed that connected Asia and North America.

The usual theory has been that people, and some animals, traveled across that "land bridge" and then south down a corridor between mountain ranges that was free of ice because it was so dry, similar to the dryness of central and eastern Oregon caused by the "rain shadow" of the Cascades. In recent years, however, another theory has been suggested. Rather than traveling on land, people may have used boats, similar to the ones used by northern people in more recent times, and traveled around the edge of the land bridge and down the West Coast past the glaciers. An ice-free corridor would have been a frozen desert, similar to areas in Siberia and Mongolia, and food would have been scarce, but fish and sea mammals were plentiful around the edges of the ice. Also, some of the oldest sites of human occupation in the New World have been found in South America.

A highly speculative idea goes a step farther. Some specialists have wondered why there couldn't have been a similar migration across the Atlantic from northern Europe around the edges of the frozen shelves of water that probably connected exposed north Atlantic islands as well as Iceland and Greenland. It could explain the four or five very old human skeletons that have been found that appear to have some Caucasian features.

But wherever indigenous people came from, and however long ago, they were successfully settled upon the land when the wave of Europeans arrived, after the New World was "discovered." They brought a different way of life from much more crowded land. To their eyes, this vast country seemed unfilled, unpopulated—it still does to many visiting Europeans—and a clash of cultures was inevitable.

In the early chapters of *This Far-Off Sunset Land,* Carolyn Buan takes that provoking concept and brings it to the personal level of the history and people of our own community. That is one reason why her pictorial history of Washington County intrigued me so. There are others.

As I drive or walk around my community, especially as it is going through a new surge of growth, random thoughts about this area often cross my mind. Why was this road put there? Why did a town develop in that particular location? Where did the names of the streets and communities come from? Who lived on my land before the woman who sold it to me? Who first lived here?

In her handsome book, Carolyn Buan answers many of those questions for the residents of Washington County. With fascinating photographs and absorbing text, she transports us through more recent times—the advent of railroads and automobiles, for example—and delivers us to the still-changing present, tracing the people and the events in this unique corner of Oregon along the way.

Jean M. Auel

Author of *Earth's Children* series beginning with *The Clan of the Cave Bear,* and resident of Washington County, Oregon

PREFACE

The task of writing a history of Washington County, Oregon, has been both delightful and frustrating—delightful because there is so much of interest to discuss and frustrating for the same reason. Washington County covers a very large area, and each community in it has a unique history. Although I have tried to be evenhanded in my coverage of major themes and events, there is much that had to be left unsaid. Indeed, I have only been able to touch on a few of the many *personal* dramas that make up the foundations of community life. For those detailed accounts, the reader must turn to the dozens of interesting local histories that fill several feet of bookshelf space at the Washington County Museum.

Those who helped me with this project have my deepest gratitude. They include Joan H. Smith and Barbara Doyle at the Washington County Historical Society; Jean Moore, past president of the Historical Society Board and chair of its Book Committee; Katie Hill, curator at the Children's Museum in Portland; Carol Gutmann, who reviewed and proofread the manuscript; Nancy Smith, Florence Vanasche, Florence Herinckx, Kathleen Palmer, George Williams, George Iwasaki, Ralph Raines, June Huserik, and the Washington County Visitors Association, who offered information and photos; historians Dr. Gordon B. Dodds, chair of the Department of History at Portland State University, and Richard P. Matthews, who reviewed the manuscript and offered helpful suggestions; Francisco J. Rangel, who took on special photography assignments; Dale Smith at the Camera Bag in Hillsboro, who reproduced most of the photos in the book and donated his services for a portion of that daunting task; Bob Moore of Moore Information, who conducted a market survey; John Pihas, president of John Pihas and Partners, Inc., who provided marketing consultation; Al Reser of Reser's Fine Foods, Inc., who arranged transportation of the books from Missouri to Oregon; Andy Bretthauer, who provided storage for the books; the *Hillsboro Argus* and Community Newspapers, Inc. (Times Publications), for coverage of the project; *The Oregonian*, Metro West edition, for featuring excerpts from the book in its "History Matters" column; and the Collins Foundation, which provided a generous grant in support of a project that truly has been a community effort.

Note to Readers: Early Washington County place names changed frequently during the settlement period. Before any villages or towns existed, the area around present-day Hillsboro was called the East Tualatin Plains and the area around Forest Grove was called the West Plains. For a time, Hillsboro (once spelled Hillsborough) was called East Tuality and Forest Grove was known as West Tuality.

Unless otherwise noted, photographs in the book are from the collections of the Washington County Museum. Photos from the Oregon Historical Society are abbreviated OHS, and those from the Tigard Area Historical and Preservation Association are abbreviated TAHPA.

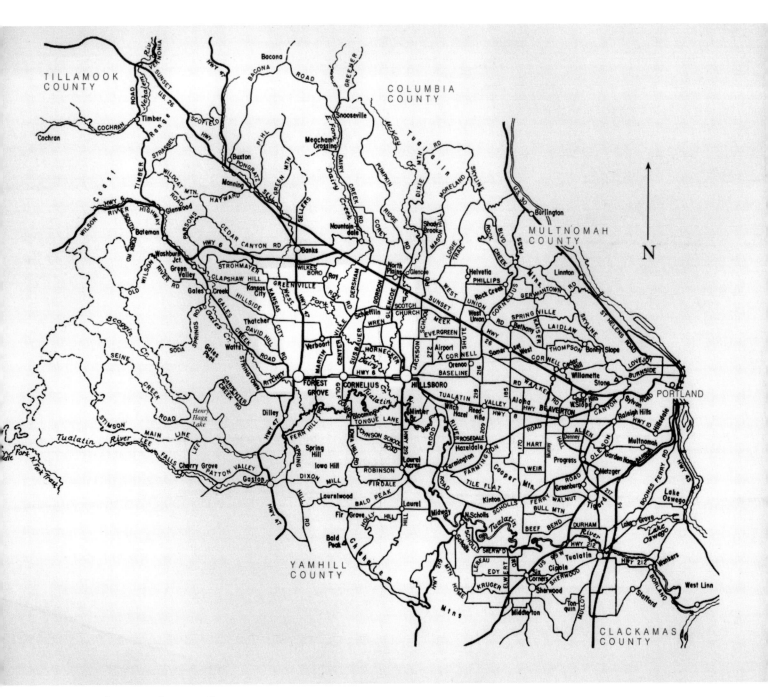

Washington County, Oregon

A. T. Smith, the first postmaster at West Tuality (Forest Grove), sits in the doorway of the log cabin that served as his post office—and probably his home. This primitive structure was uncovered by lumberyard workers in the 1930s.

INTRODUCTION

Planning a new museum facility during a 1979 fundraising campaign are State Senator Tom Hartung, the campaign's general chairman; Pat Graham, president of the Washington County Historical Society; Joan H. Smith, steering committee chair; Governor Victor Atiyeh, honorary chair; and Richard P. Matthews, museum director.

One day, during the depths of the Great Depression, workers at the Carnation Lumber Company south of Forest Grove were clearing a blackberry thicket when they uncovered a crude log building that had once been the area's first post office. Like so many of us, they were awed by the chance to touch and feel a remnant of their town's earliest history.

Even when we are lucky enough to literally "touch" the past—as those workers did—its meaning often eludes us. The earliest written accounts offer glimpses of life in the days when farmers sank their plows into the Tualatin Valley's rich soil by day and worried about marauding wolves and "panthers" by night. But those same accounts are often maddeningly vague about the hopes, fears, and aspirations of those who wove the essential fabric of Washington County life.

Fortunately, the descendants of the early settlers were determined to preserve the county's history. Over the years they established various organizations that eventually grew into the Washington County Historical Society and

Museum, now housed in a modern building on the Rock Creek campus of Portland Community College.

Today, the Museum's riches—built on a private collection donated in the early 1930s by Albert Tozier and Edyth Tozier Weatherred—include thousands of books, documents, maps, photographs, artifacts, and memorabilia that have informed much of the story you are about to read. Those treasures helped me gain some important insights about the people and events that shaped the county and the growth that in recent years has threatened to erase many traces of the past.

CHAPTER ONE

FOLLOWING ANCIENT TRAILS

For eight thousand to ten thousand years before either Europeans or Americans arrived in Oregon's western valleys, those lands were occupied by aboriginal peoples about whom very little is known. By the time of white contact, however, ten divisions of Kalapuya Indians had established recognized territories in the Willamette Valley as far south as the Umpqua watershed in southern Oregon. Among their number were several bands of Tualatins (or Atfalatis) who lived in what would later become Washington County. (Minor et al., pp. 51–52)

Left:

A rare glimpse of a Kalapuya hunter in traditional dress is afforded by an artist who came to Oregon with the Wilkes Expedition of 1838–42. The artist noted that the man "wore moccasins, an elk-skin dress, a cap of fox-skin with the ears remaining, and his quiver was of seal-skin."

Our first glimpse of the Kalapuyans comes from Alexander Henry, a fur trader for the Canadian-based North West Company who stayed near the falls of the Willamette River (now Oregon City) in 1814 and recorded his observations in his diary. Accustomed to the fierce mounted warriors and large tribes to the east, Henry considered the Kalapuyans "a wretched tribe."

[They are] an ugly, ill-formed race, and four of them had some defect of the eyes. . . . Those we met were wretchedly clothed in deerskins; their quivers were of deer's heads and necks. Their women had petticoats of fringed leather, like the Chinook women's cedar petticoats, but reaching only halfway down the thighs. They wore small round bonnets of wattap . . . with a peak three inches high. They were of short stature, and altogether the most miserable, wild, and rascally looking tribe I have seen on this side of the Rocky Mountains. (Mackey, p. 2)

Another account described the Kalapuyans as having "broad, flat, fleshy noses, with low bridges and unusually large nostrils," wide mouths, thick lips, and excellent teeth, which wore down with age from eating food that contained sand. (Mackey, p. 4) According to one account, they loved finery and often wore red feathers on their heads, hung beads from their necks and ears, and suspended dentalium shells from their noses. Atfalati women wore a skirt or apron of tanned hide or grasses and were barebreasted or wore a deer-skin chemise. Unlike some Willamette Valley groups, the Tualatins did not tattoo themselves, but those of high status had flattened foreheads. (Mackey, pp. 22–23)

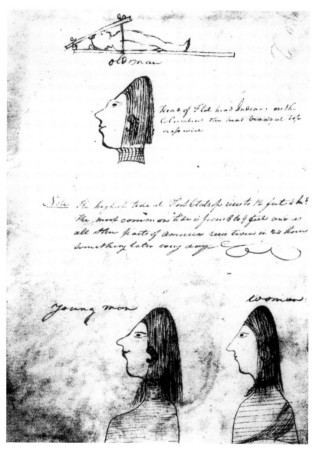

A flattened forehead was a sign of high status for some groups of Indians, including the Kalapuyans. These sketches of Indians along the Columbia River were made by Meriwether Lewis during the Lewis and Clark Expedition of 1804–06. (OHS Neg. 645)

Food Sources

The Tualatins lived primarily on roots, nuts, and berries gathered in a predictable "seasonal round" that took them to the same spots year after year. In spring, summer, and fall, bands of two or three families roamed in search of food, gathering at their traditional campsites where they slept out under huge pines and cedars or in brush-and-pole structures covered with fir boughs. From eyewitness accounts, we know that some of their campsites were located at the "Five Oaks" north of Hillsboro and others were near Bethany and Mountaindale, where they hunted waterfowl. (Benson, p. 6)

The seasonal round began in January, as the Atfalati fished for steelhead in the valley's rivers and streams. In April through July, they visited Willamette Falls to fish or trade for salmon, and from July to December they caught fall chinook, silvers, and chums. In June the women and children gathered berries, which grew in great profusion throughout the valley; in July and August they gathered hazelnuts and caterpillars. In the fall, some bands moved into the hills to hunt for elk and deer, while others stayed in the valley to gather the wapato, a tuber that grew in the marshes and lakes. The most important item in their diet, however, was the camas, an onion-like bulb that was harvested from spring to fall. Once roasted, the camas bulbs were ground and made into thick, moist cakes that could be stored throughout the winter or used as a principal trade item. (Minor, et al., pp. 56–59)

One of the Kalapuyans' most important food-gathering techniques was prairie burning, a practice that made it easier to harvest tarweed. Using hoops that resembled tennis rackets, the women beat the tarweed pods to make the seeds drop into large platters. Then they parched and ground the seeds in a stone mortar, sometimes mixing them with mashed, cooked camas, and hazelnuts. (Zenk, pp. 58–59). Prairie burning also made it easier to harvest grasshoppers, hunt deer, and maintain the vast open spaces that were needed for camas to grow.

Shelter

During the rainy winters, the Tualatins lived in twenty-three permanent villages dotted around Wapato Lake (near present-day Gaston), and in the areas that later became Forest Grove, Hillsboro, and Beaverton. (Minor et al., pp. 52–53) Their long houses were built of poles covered with planks, large pieces of bark, or twisted bundles of grass mounted on wood frames. Inside was a central fireplace with a hole in the roof where smoke could escape. Around the fireplace were separate living areas, partitioned with cattail mats and outfitted with sleeping platforms. (Beckham, p. 45)

Sociopolitical Organization and Customs

Although information about early social organization is sketchy, some accounts suggest that each village may have had a headman, or chief (either a man or a woman chosen because of wealth), as well as a village council. (Zenk, p. 16) Kalapuyan

Although the Tualatin Indians often subsisted on roots, nuts, and berries, they sometimes visited the falls of the Willamette River to trade wapato and smoke-dried meat for the abundant salmon their wealthier neighbors caught there. The traditional method of fishing with dipnets was captured by Joseph Drayton in this 1841 sketch. (OHS Neg. 46193)

The Tualatin Valley in 1841 was a broad open plain, kept free of underbrush by the Indians' practice of prairie burning. When the fires died down, the women could quickly harvest the tarweed seed, an important food source. However, some areas were left green to attract deer and make hunting easier. (OHS Neg. 46191)

groups that occupied the same general territory (for example, the Tualatins and Yamhills) shared similar dress and customs. However, communication between various groups sometimes required the help of an interpreter. (Beckham, p. 45)

All the Tualatins shared certain harvest places (like the north end of Wapato Lake), while individual bands were allotted specific sites. (Zenk, p. 17) Between the Tualatins and other groups, boundaries existed, along with understandings of where crossings could be made. Klickitats, for example, made journeys into Tualatin territory to hunt, and many groups from around the region gathered at certain trading spots like Willamette Falls to exchange foods. (Zenk, p. 47ff.)

Families traced their ancestry through the father's side, and marriages were made outside the village. (Wealthy men could have several wives.) Slaves, purchased or captured during raids to the south and along the coast, could marry other slaves held by the same owner—or even marry free persons—as long as the owner received horses in payment. Such payments also ensured the slaves' later freedom. The children of marriages between slaves were also slaves, but they were usually not sold outside that family.

Religious Beliefs

The Atfalati apparently believed in a divine being called *Ay-uthlme-i*, which means "miraculous." According to an early Willamette Valley physician, Dr. W. W. Oglesby, the Kalapuyans also believed in a kind of heaven and hell, where a person went as a result of his behavior on earth. The doctor's informant, a chief, stressed that his people

A typical winter dwelling was a long house that accommodated several families. Like the Tualatins' dwellings, the Chinook long house pictured here has a fireplace, sleeping platforms, and meat hung overhead to cure. (OHS Neg. 4465)

considered lying the greatest crime, one that resulted in severe punishment. (Mackey, pp. 22 and 26)

Like many other Native Americans, the Kalapuyans believed that each individual was guided by spirit powers, which could bring good or bad luck, give strength, and govern the course of one's life. These powers were acquired at puberty by going to special holy places and undergoing five days of fasting and other prescribed activities.

The End of a Culture

When Alexander Henry observed the Kalapuyans in 1814, he reported them to be a large nation, but they had been a much larger one before 1782–83 when a smallpox epidemic had destroyed an estimated two thousand of their number. By the 1840s, when settlers began to arrive, the Kalapuyans had been decimated by other epidemics, including an outbreak of fever from 1830 to 1833 that wiped out between seven-eighths and nine-tenths of the region's native inhabitants. (Minor et al, p. 102)

The few Tualatins who were left (an estimated six hundred in 1842 and sixty in 1848) sometimes helped the settlers find food during their early months in Oregon. But in years to come the Tualatins were reduced to begging for food. When that happened, some were turned away through ignorance and fear, but others were accommodated. Each year the Wilkes family on the North Tualatin Plains welcomed the Indians back to their old camp to harvest hazelnuts and acorns; William Walker, an early settler in Cedar Mill, allowed them to harvest wild fruit on his donation land

"The Five Oaks" in the northern Tualatin Valley was a summer camp the Atfalatis visited each year. Later, retired trappers and other pioneers held their Fourth of July picnics, religious revivals, horse races, and county court sessions here.

claim; and John Rowell, near Scholl's Ferry, let them camp and fish on his land. (Fulton, p. 10; Brody and Olson, pp. 7 and 9; Hesse, pp. 2–3)

While most settlers lived peacefully with the Indians, pitied their condition, or ignored them, a few lodged complaints. Once, a small band, deprived of camas and game and on the point of starvation, killed an ox and nearly triggered an outbreak of violence. Another time, the Reverend John Smith Griffin went so far as to build a private jail in which to incarcerate Indians when they stole small items from him. (Bourke and DeBats, p. 43)

In 1850–51, when a treaty was finally negotiated with the local Indians, they were promised a paltry $500 each year for twenty years, plus blankets, clothing, and tools, and were granted a small reservation at Wapato Lake. However, while that agreement was being negotiated, Congress abrogated the treaty commission's powers, rendering the treaty null and void. In 1855 a new treaty was drawn up that removed the Tualatins to a new reservation at Grand Ronde, leaving their homeland to the settlers.

At Grand Ronde, the Tualatins were thrown together with members of other Indian groups whose languages they could not understand. There they lived for several decades, intermarrying with other groups, learning the white man's ways, and gradually losing their cultural identity.

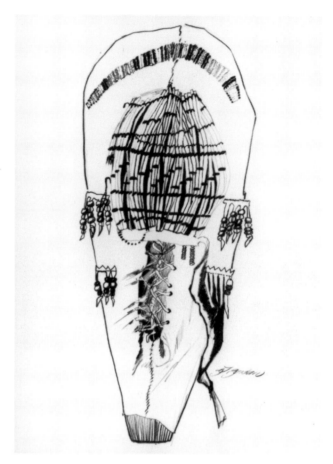

This papoose board, sketched by Jennifer Jordan, was given to her pioneer grandmother, Mary Hall Reeves, by an Indian woman.

At Wapato Lake, just east of present-day Gaston, the Tualatins had several permanent winter villages. During treaty negotiations in 1850–51, they asked to have a reservation established here. That request was denied and in 1855 a new treaty provided for a reservation at Grand Ronde. Later, the American settlers drained Wapato Lake and created the "Gaston Ditch" for irrigation purposes. (Courtesy of George Williams)

The Indian School in Forest Grove

The plight of Pacific Northwest Indians weighed heavily on some of the settlers, who believed that the natives' only hope was to learn the white man's ways. In 1879 Pacific University wrote to the U.S. government offering the community of Forest Grove as the site for an Indian Training School that would draw students from tribes throughout the Pacific Northwest. The offer was accepted, and two years later the new school's superintendent, Captain M. C. Wilkinson, could report that the pupils had cleared a site, built the first building, and begun to learn useful occupations. Although some townspeople reacted negatively to the school, others made the children feel welcome. Indeed, the school was so successful it outgrew its location a few blocks from the university (between present-day Twenty-second and Twenty-third and C and D Streets). When additional contiguous land could not be found, the government moved the school to Salem, where it still operates today under the name *Chemawa*.

The student body of the Indian Training School in Forest Grove gathers for a group portrait. The Training School was part of a federal program to improve the lot of Indian children by preparing them for white society. The building at the right was erected by the students themselves.

Misery and resentment are evident in the faces of these children, who were forcibly removed from their homes and required to abandon their native dress, speech, and customs.

Shoemaking was one of the trades for which the boys were prepared, while the girls learned the domestic arts.

CHAPTER TWO

ANOTHER WORLD INTRUDES

Immigrants arriving over the Oregon Trail were not the first outsiders to settle among the Indians of the Willamette and Tualatin Valleys. The authors of *Cultural Resource Overview of BLM Lands in Northwestern Oregon* have traced a series of encounters that introduced the Kalapuyans to Euro-Americans and their ways. (Minor et al., pp. 100ff.)

Early Encounters

Those encounters began in 1811, when a small party of fur traders from John Jacob Astor's Pacific Fur Company at Fort Astoria entered the Willamette Valley intent on establishing a post.

Left:

Joseph Meek—seen here in full regalia—was one of a small group of former fur trappers who moved to the Tualatin Valley in December 1840 to begin farming on the North Tualatin Plains. They were soon joined by an odd assortment of missionaries, Hudson's Bay Company workers, and overland immigrants.

That party was followed in 1812–13 by two others and by the establishment of a "trading house" in what was probably the vicinity of Salem. Other groups continued to travel through the area, and in 1826 a party from the British Hudson's Bay Company, headquartered at Fort Vancouver on the Columbia River, passed through the Yamhill Valley and across the Tualatin Plains.

In the years after 1829, settlement began in the areas north and south of the Plains, as French Canadians from the North West and Hudson's Bay Companies retired and established farms. Then in 1834 Methodist missionary Jason Lee founded a mission just north of present-day Salem, and his workers soon began farming nearby.

By 1840, when the first non-Indian settlers moved onto the Tualatin Plains, the Kalapuyans were familiar with the fur traders, had seen herdsmen from Fort Vancouver pasture their cattle on the prairies, and had acquired some of the white man's goods.

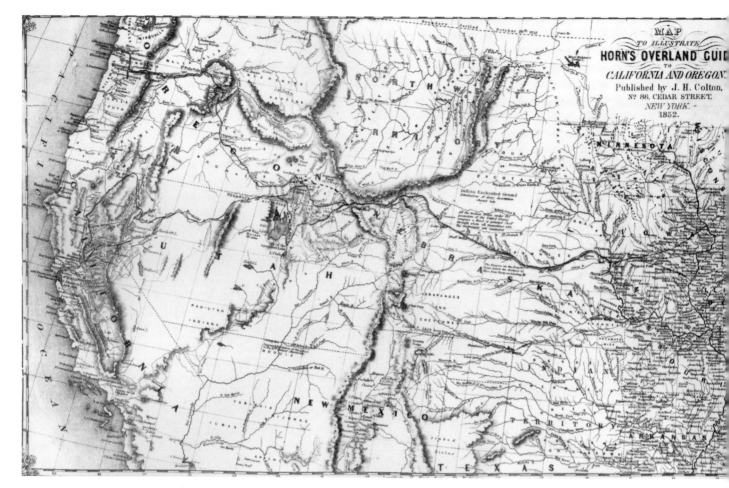

Mountain Men— The First Settlers

The first outsiders to settle in the Tualatin Valley were a group of independent American fur trappers who had been forced by a dwindling beaver population to abandon their nomadic existence in the Rocky Mountains and seek a new way to support their Indian wives and children. With some trepidation, they made their way to the vast Oregon Country, where they soon discovered that the only avenue open to them was farming.

As one of them—the colorful Joe Meek—later recalled, the Hudson's Bay Company had a near monopoly on farming supplies: "Some they furnished with supplies, some they did not. . . . If a man would take a claim, he could get seed wheat,

This map, published for wagon train migrants, shows the vast reach of the old Oregon Country. (OHS Neg. Orhi 26235)

ploughs, hoes, harrows, teeth, and so on, if he would show a disposition to go to work to raise wheat, which they was the only market for." (Tobie, p. 94) Dr. John McLoughlin, the company's chief factor, also made sure that the mountain men—who were given to drinking, gambling, and womanizing—settled as far away from the region's missionaries and traders as possible.

Christmastime 1840 saw Joe Meek, Robert Newell, Courtney Walker, William Doughty, Caleb Wilkins, and their families camped in leaky leather Indian lodges at the foot of Chehalem Mountain, near a small cabin that Doughty had

In 1824 the British Hudson's Bay Company established a fur trading post, Fort Vancouver, on the northern bank of the Columbia River near the mouth of the Willamette. Until the mid-1840s—when American settlers began to fill up the western valleys—the company's chief factor, Dr. John McLoughlin, ruled the region with a firm but benign hand. (OHS Neg. Orhi 9257)

Left:
All the "Rocky Mountain Boys" who settled on the Tualatin Plains had Indian wives. Virginia Meek, wife of Joseph Meek, was a Nez Perce Indian who often longed for her people but remained in the Tualatin Valley, to become a respected member of the community.

acquired during an earlier visit. There they remained during the long winter, soaked to the skin and subsisting almost entirely on boiled wheat. Miraculously, they survived, and the next spring began to stake out their claims. They were soon joined by two other mountain men, "Squire" George Wood Ebbert and Joseph Gale.

Missionaries and Red River Settlers

By the summer of 1841, the mountain men had invited a radical Congregationalist—John Smith Griffin—and his wife Desiré to settle among them and minister to them. Griffin had planned to establish an Indian mission east of the Cascades, but his request for missionary board support had been denied, he had failed to find any Indians to minister to, and now he and his wife were nearly destitute. Fortunately, as he and other settlers were to learn, the Tualatin Indians' practice of burning the prairie had cleared away brush and grass, leaving its rich black soil ready for the plow. With supplies from the Hudson's Bay Company, Griffin was able to relocate and, within a few years, to establish a prosperous farm.

In addition to the retired mountain men and their families, Griffin's flock soon included a handful of Hudson's Bay Company workers and their families, known as the Red River settlers. These families, from the Red River region of what is now Manitoba, Canada, had been sent to the Pacific Northwest to farm in the Puget Sound area, but poor soil and insensitive treatment by Hudson's Bay Company overseers had caused them to move

to the fertile Tualatin Valley. There, they began to farm and quickly made friends with the mountain men who preceded them.

The Red River men were James Birston; Henry Buxton Jr. and Henry Buxton Sr.; Horatio Colder; John, James, and David Flett; Henry King; John Johnson; Charles Richard McKay; David Munroe; Thomas Otchin; Michael Wren; and William Baldra. These men—and many of their wives—were Anglo-métis, which means that they were of mixed Scots, English, and Indian blood. Later, other Red River settlers arrived, and by 1860 many of them were among the wealthiest settlers on the Tualatin Plains. (Bourke and DeBats, p. 49)

Like the mountain men, the Red River men were an earthy, fun-loving bunch, whose habits horrified the Reverend Griffin. Many had taken Indian wives without benefit of clergy—a situation the minister determined to correct—and many enjoyed dancing. Even before Griffin's work began, the stage was set for a parting of the ways.

More Missionaries

No sooner had the Griffins staked out their new mission field than they were joined by another group of independent Congregational missionaries, led by the Reverend Harvey Clark. Clark's small mission party consisted of his wife Emeline, Alvin (A. T.) and Abigail Smith, and P. B. and Adelaide Littlejohn. Like the Griffins, this group had stopped at the Protestant mission of Marcus and Narcissa Whitman near present-day Walla Walla, Washington; visited with other missionaries in the area; and found that all the mission fields

In 1841 the Reverend John Smith Griffin and his wife Desiré accepted an invitation to settle among the mountain men. Griffin formally established his tiny First Congregational Church of Tualatin Plains on June 26, 1842.

Among Reverend Griffin's parishioners were the Red River settlers, former employees of the Hudson's Bay Company. Charles McKay (left) established the town of Glencoe, and Thomas Otchin took up a land claim north of Orenco.

among the large Indian tribes east of the Cascade Mountains had been taken. Their last hope was a mission to the Tualatin Indians, but for several reasons that effort was doomed.

Both Clark and Griffin had been caught up in the missionary zeal of "The Second Great Awakening," a rebirth of religious fervor that swept the country in the early nineteenth century. At Oberlin Institute in the Ohio wilderness, they had been inspired by the famous revivalist Charles Finney, who told his students, "nobody was fit to be a missionary who was not willing with but an ear of corn in his pocket to start for the Rocky Mountains." (Buan, p. 4) As a result, his students undertook their missions ill-prepared, underfunded, and unaware that the Indians were semino-madic and little disposed to accept Christianity. Imbued with the belief that farming was a godly occupation, the missionaries would try—but fail—to get the Indians to till the soil.

When the Clark party reached the Tualatin Valley, the men had only one month to build a shelter for three families before the fall rains began. Worse yet, they had no food to sustain them through the long winter. While Smith, a skilled carpenter, struggled in the unending downpours to build a mission house, the Clarks and Littlejohns moved to Salem, where Clark taught for the Methodists, helped missionary Jason Lee establish the school that was to become Willamette University, and taught some children in his own tiny cabin. The next spring, after a few halfhearted attempts to minister to the Tualatins, Smith and Clark decided to abandon their mission.

While Smith remained on the mission site along the Tualatin River on the West Tualatin Plains (the area in and around present-day Forest Grove) and expanded his farm, Clark moved to the East Plains (the Hillsboro area) and ministered to the mountain men and Red River settlers, who by that time had become disenchanted with the Reverend Griffin's joyless ways. The Clarks' home was in what would soon become the tiny crossroads settlement of Glencoe, a town whose remnants still can be seen near North Plains.

Oregon Trail Migrants

As the handful of families on the Tualatin Plains farmed, journeyed to Fort Vancouver for supplies, and held religious meetings in one another's cabins, a movement was afoot that would swell their numbers. For years, reports had been published in the East that pictured the Oregon Country as having a healthful climate, ample rainfall, fertile soil, and great beauty. These reports held special appeal for farmers in the Mississippi, Ohio, and Missouri River Valleys, many of whom had only recently left their homes in the eastern and southern parts of the country and pioneered on that new frontier. Among those attracted to Oregon were adventurers who liked the prospect of living in a wilderness, skilled craftsmen from the North looking for a new place to live, and large extended Southern families. The latter had already made a series of moves together and would move again as a group, to settle in the same neighborhood at the end of the Oregon Trail.

Some of those who eventually journeyed to the Tualatin Valley had first left the Southern states

First Families. *Among the rare photographs of early settlers, now in the collection of the Washington County Museum, are (clockwise, from top left) those of Isaiah and Winifred Kelsey (Hillsboro area), Samuel and Naomi Oliver Walters (Cedar Mill), and James and Mary Cornelius Imbrie (Hillsboro area).*

because they detested slavery, either because of ethical objections or because they knew firsthand that it led to a scarcity of land and to social relations that were "hierarchical and oppressive." (Bourke and DeBats, p. 67) Others resented the slaves because they represented a cheap form of labor with which poor white farmers could not compete.

For many, the final move to Oregon was triggered by an economic crisis (the Panic of 1837), falling prices, and floods that dominated life in the Mississippi, Missouri, and Ohio River Valleys and left families without the means to pay the mortgages on their farms—or without any farms at all. For others, the move was made to avoid the devastating outbreaks of malaria, influenza, smallpox, and scarlet fever that had raged for years in those valleys. The prospect of a healthy climate—coupled with the rumor that the government might soon give 320 acres of land to each man and 320 to each married woman—was enough to make them undertake the arduous overland trek to Oregon. And it was enough to make many farmers marry hastily before they began the journey—or marry girls as young as thirteen and fourteen once they arrived in Oregon.

Historian Robert Benson once tried to list the Oregon Trail migrants who arrived in Washington County each year. For the first few years of migration, he was able to verify the families' names, but later years' listings are incomplete—in part because early compilations were also incomplete, in part because settlers often failed to specify the year in which they traveled to Oregon.

In 1841 only three "American stragglers" arrived over the Oregon Trail: David Hill (for whom Hillsboro was later named), Isaiah Kelsey, and Richard "Irish Dick" Williams. They settled on the East Plains. In 1842 Benson lists William Bennett, A. N. Coats, Archibald Spence, and Philip Thompson, as well as Henry Black and Walter Pomeroy, who moved to the area from elsewhere in Oregon.

A large number of migrants reached the Tualatin Valley in 1843, settling on the West and East Plains. They included (on the West Plains) Richard Arthur, Orus Brown, Solomon Emerick, William Geiger, Thomas Naylor, William Wilson, Almoran Hill, John Mills, and Jacob Reed and (on the East Plains) William Beagle, Reverend James Cave, Riley Cave, Edward Constable, John B. Jackson, David T. Lenox, Edward Lenox, Louise Lenox, William Mauzey, Henry Sewell, Anderson Smith, Isaac Smith, John G. White, Joseph W. Woods, Alexander Zachary, and John Q. Zachary.

The next year brought only James Gerrish, Alanson Hinman, Jacob Hoover, John Lousignont, Michael Moore, Wesley Mulkey, W. G. Scoggin, and Benjamin Q. Tucker, but 1845 saw another large migration. After 1845 migrations of varying sizes continued to come for many years.

A Time of Isolation

As the first families moved into the Tualatin Valley, they had their pick of the finest prairie land—or land that combined forest and open meadows. During this period, the settlers' large land holdings kept them isolated from one another. On the eastern edge of the future Washington County, Augustus Fanno and his son lived a lonely life from 1847 until 1850, when Augustus persuaded Thomas and Berrilla Denney to settle nearby. That year, Lawrence Hall filed his land claim in the area that would become Beaverton, David C. Graham settled his claim to the southeast, and the Denneys' cousins, the Hicklins, settled near what would become Tigard. Two years later, Wilson M. Tigard, for whom that city is named, settled near his brother's donation land claim. (See Mapes, *Chakeipi*.) Meanwhile Samuel Walters had filed his claim in 1848 in the area that would become Cedar Mill—his nearest neighbors, the Walker family on what is now Walker Road.

The Goal: Survival

In those early years, the goal was survival. Many came unprepared to support themselves, so those who came first had to help members of the next year's migration. As Peter Burnett, a Tualatin Valley settler (and later governor of California) recounted:

. . . There were no hotels in the country, as there was nothing wherewith to pay the bills. The oldest settlers had necessarily to throw open their doors to the new immigrants, and entertain them free of charge. Our houses were small log cabins, and our bedding was scarce. The usual mode of travel was for each one to carry his blankets with him, and sleep upon the puncheon floor. Our families were often overworked in waiting upon others, and our provisions vanished before the keen appetites of our new guests. "They bred a famine wherever they went."

According to Burnett, settlers—by necessity—were an upright lot:

They were all honest, because there was nothing to steal; they were all sober, because there was no liquor to drink; there were no misers, because there was no money to hoard, and they were all industrious, because it was work or starve. (p. 174)

In the absence of money, the settlers borrowed wheat from one another, exchanged wheat for clothing, or asked for credit from the Hudson's Bay Company. When they were able, they repaid their loans in wheat. Even when other stores were established and goods could be had, many things the settlers needed were not available or were too expensive. But within a few years, as the local economy improved, roads were built, and harvests found ready markets, those problems disappeared and many of the settlers could lead quite comfortable lives.

At first, however, they had to haul logs from nearby forests to build their homes and barns—and often to craft crude furniture and tools. The task of sawing the logs into boards and splitting shingles for roofs was arduous, and as a result the first houses were primitive log structures. Soon, though, a few enterprising men set up small sawmills on their property, where farmers in the area could bring logs to be sawn into boards. By the 1850s, more refined houses—usually in the Classical Revival style—began to appear.

An early sawmill proprietor (1844) was Joseph Gale, who set his mill up on Gales Creek. Other mills were built by Henry Davis on McKay Creek (just west of the Hillsboro Cemetery, 1848), Peter

To help break the Hudson Bay Company's monopoly on livestock, Tualatin Valley settler Joseph Gale and five other men built The Star of Oregon. In September 1842 he sailed the 53-foot schooner to California, where he sold it and used the proceeds to buy cattle. The next year, he returned to Oregon with forty-two new immigrants and their herds of 1,250 head of cattle, six hundred horses and mules, and three thousand sheep. (OHS Neg. Orhi 76419)

Logs for the first houses in the Tualatin Valley came from the pioneers' donation land claims. Long after Dr. Wilson Bowlby built a frame house in Forest Grove, his family continued to harvest timber from his claim. Seen here in 1899 are (second and third from the left) Charles and Theodore Bowlby. At the far right is William Pitman.

Scholl and James M. Rowell (in the area now known as Scholls, 1849), and Thomas Denney, for whom Denney Road is named, on Fanno Creek a short time later.

Besides sawmills, the settlers needed places to grind their grain into flour, and gristmills quickly sprang up around the valley. One was built by John Jackson on Jackson's Creek and another by William O. Gibson near Gaston. For the most part, however, farm families were largely self-sufficient and life was relatively uncomplicated. But that would soon begin to change.

Sawmills made it possible for the pioneers to abandon their log houses and barns for the more sophisticated building styles they had left in the Midwest and East. This old sawmill, owned and operated by William Henry Williams and his son Charlie, was photographed west of Forest Grove near Watts in the early 1950s.

One old mill was Butler's, which operated for many years near present-day Orenco.

Clearing the forested areas after the trees were cut was a time-consuming operation that involved burning the stumps. Using much the same technique, circa 1920, two men from Mountaindale have drilled holes in the centers of logs and filled them with flammable powder.

*The settlers' first log houses were quickly aban-
doned in favor of more sophisticated construction
and styles. John E. Campbell built this Vernacular
Classical Revival house in 1852 near Laurel. The
house is pictured in 1911.*

Mary Walker (seated) and her husband Elkanah were missionaries to the Nez Perce in what is now Idaho until an Indian uprising at the nearby Whitman Mission made their work too dangerous. They later moved to West Tuality (Forest Grove), where they helped build the Congregational Church and Tualatin Academy. Mary is seen here with her grown children at their home—reputedly the first frame house in Forest Grove.

In the late 1800s, interest in Washington County
pioneers ran high. When Fourth of July celebrations became common, Oregon Trail migrants of
the 1840s and 1850s were persuaded to ride on
special wagons in parades. Pictured, from left,
are William Adams, an unidentified man, S. D.
Powell, Calvin and Catherine Adams, J. P. Butler,
Mrs. S. Holcomb, an unidentified woman, Mrs.
Butler, Mrs. Sam Williams, and Mike Moore.

CHAPTER THREE

ESTABLISHING A GOVERNMENT

Many American settlers in Oregon distrusted the British government (represented by the Hudson's Bay Company) and wanted to form a government that would safeguard their property interests. In 1843 several Tualatin Valley men joined with other Oregon settlers to organize a provisional government that could function until the British and American governments could establish a border and decide, once and for all, the question of who would possess Oregon.

Left:

A tale of frontier government is told in this early-twentieth-century photograph of the County Courthouse in Hillsboro. In 1891, as county business increased, this handsome clock tower was added to the existing 1873 brick building. Although a well-known architect, Delos Neer, was hired to design the addition, the county was unable to raise enough money to replace the clock's "temporary" false face.

A Strong Showing from the Tualatin Plains

Tualatin Valley men were very much in evidence at Champoeg, where the meeting to approve a provisional government was held. Although reports of the meeting vary, it appears that Harvey Clark, William Doughty, George Ebbert, Joseph Gale, John Smith Griffin, David Hill, Charles McKay, Joe Meek, and Robert Newell were present and voted for the new government. A. T. Smith and Caleb Wilkins presumably voted yes too, although some evidence suggests they did not actually attend the meeting.

The three-member executive committee of the new government included two men from the Tualatin Plains, David Hill and Joseph Gale. Charles McKay was chosen captain; A. T. Smith magistrate, and George Ebbert constable. Later, Peter Burnett (a lawyer) became supreme judge. The Legislative Committee, which served until 1845, included twelve men—of whom five (David Hill, Robert Newell, William Doughty, Peter Burnett, and Joe Meek) were from the Tualatin Plains.

The need for some form of government in the Oregon Country led to several meetings, including this gathering at Champoeg on May 2, 1843. Among the Tualatin Valley men who took part in the meeting was Joe Meek, seen waving his hat (center) as he called for the vote that established a provisional government. His neighbor, Reverend John Griffin, is pictured behind him on the right. (OHS Neg. Orhi 394)

The Boundary Question

The next year the thorny matter of establishing a boundary between English and American territory was finally negotiated, and in the Anglo-American Treaty of 1846 the boundary was set at the forty-ninth parallel. In 1848 Congress made Oregon a territory, and in 1850 the Oregon Donation Land Act was passed. These events allayed the settlers' concerns that their land might come under British control or that their full land claims might not be recognized by the United States government. Each man and wife who settled in Oregon before 1853 could claim 640 acres, assuring that the area would remain rural and fairly sparsely settled for some time to come.

The Beginnings of a County

When the provisional government was established, the Oregon Country was divided into four administrative districts, of which Tuality was one. This district was large, covering an area that stretched from the Yamhill River to 54° 40' and from the Willamette River to the Pacific Ocean. At first, it had no district seat, and for the first months of the provisional government's existence, court sessions were held at the small meeting house that stood on the Edward Constable claim (just off the Sunset Highway, near what is now NW 253rd Avenue). However, due perhaps to the influence of David Hill—a member of the Provisional Government Legislative Committee and a New England man with aspirations beyond farming—the seat of government grew up on Hill's East Plains land claim. He sold forty acres of his claim and a small log building to the court for $200, indicating that the court should plat a town there and call it Columbus. The cabin was to serve as a Courthouse and, according to one account, the first jury room was a log "to which the jurors retired to whittle and arrive at a verdict." After Hill's death in 1850, Columbus was renamed Hillsborough in his honor. (Matthews, pp. 104ff.)

In 1846 the district of Tuality became Tuality County, and in 1849 the territorial legislature changed the county name from Tuality to Washington. During the first half of the 1850s, county boundaries were redrawn several times to accommodate other newly created counties. But in 1855 Washington County assumed a shape approximating its present configuration, and

Joseph Gale (top) and "Squire" George Wood Ebbert (bottom), two of the "Rocky Mountain Boys," were drawn into the provisional government—Gale as one of three members of the Executive Committee and Ebbert as constable. Ebbert was a blacksmith by trade and Gale a grist and sawmill operator.

county government began in earnest under a three-member Board of Commissioners that had been formed in 1853.

A second Courthouse had been built in 1852 on land donated by Isaiah and Winifred Kelsey and the county had sold lots in the newly platted town of Hillsborough, aided by the promotional rhetoric of Abraham Sulger, the only merchant in town. His advertisements in the *Oregon Spectator* were designed to attract other businessmen to the East Plains, which was populated by farmers who apparently had little interest in urban pursuits. As Richard Matthews explains, the first offering of town lots yielded twelve sales—three to Sulger himself, two to Dr. Ralph Wilcox, one to Michael Moore, a neighboring farmer, and the rest to A. T. Smith, William Geiger Sr., William Geiger Jr., David Lenox, and George Ebbert. The latter were men from elsewhere in the county who either held county government posts or had a strong interest in public affairs. These lots clustered around a public square, and many remained vacant for some time to come. (Matthews, pp. 109ff.)

Thus, Hillsborough grew slowly and remained for several years a "town" in name only, providing little in the way of goods or services to the surrounding farming community. It was a place that filled up on special occasions like the Fourth of July, election day, days when court was in session, and days when other county business had to be conducted; but at other times it saw little activity. (Bourke and DeBats, p. 320)

By 1860 the settlement could claim only twelve families and a handful of businesses— two stores, one hotel, two blacksmiths, and two wagoners, as well as a doctor, a lawyer, and a bookkeeper. Richard Matthews attributes the lack of growth over the next twenty-five years in part to a lack of ambition among the townspeople, but he notes that the settlement's location away from a

riverbank and main roads was also a factor. (Matthews, Chap. 7) Only after railroad service began in the 1870s did Hillsboro begin to grow and serve the surrounding farming community to any appreciable degree.

For many years the county seat remained a sleepy hamlet that offered but few amenities. Among them was the Tualatin Hotel (right), built in 1852, a farmer's exchange, a billiard hall, and a livery stable.

The Business of Governing

County government in its early years was concerned with setting taxes, operating the courts and a law enforcement system, building roads, establishing schools, taking care of paupers, and holding elections. In fact, the daily business of government involved the settlers very directly, and many of them helped build roads, petitioned to set up schools, acted as school officers, and performed other duties.

Where road building was concerned, county government facilitated the process, ensured fairness, and bore some of the costs. The county provided surveyors and road district supervisors, but the citizens did the physical work. A major incentive for the county and its citizens was the avoidance of unnecessary expense, for few people had any money to spare. Those who took on leadership positions (18 percent of the male population in 1857–58) also found the fees they received to be welcome additions to their family incomes. (Bourke and DeBats, pp. 104–107)

The county's executive branch included three popularly elected commissioners, a sheriff, and a county auditor. This executive group—like those who held other positions—served only part time and met infrequently. (Bourke and DeBats, p. 95)

Law Enforcement

The residents of Washington County—and indeed Oregon as a whole—were familiar with the circuit-riding style of law enforcement personified in the 1840s by the irrepressible Joe Meek—first as sheriff for the provisional government and then as

The first jail to serve Washington County was this cramped log cabin, commissioned in 1853. Today, it stands on the Washington County Fairgrounds—a rare example of hewn-log construction from the early settlement period and the oldest public building in the county.

U.S. marshal. For many years after the office of county sheriff was established, law enforcement was conducted in a similar way, as described by Sheriff Jesse Moore in a November 20, 1867 letter to his family in Arkansas.

I am in danger by Tom, Dick, and Harry, and have a great many things to look after in all parts of the county, and frequently in three or four other counties. I have just returned from a trip of over two hundred miles ride, after a horse thief. The most of my time is engaged in official duty.

That "duty" was indeed daunting. Among other things, the sheriff served civil summonses, subpoenaed witnesses, conducted foreclosures, executed liens, held prisoners in the County Jail or transported them to the penitentiary, executed death sentences, took the census, enforced laws prohibiting the sale of liquor to Indians, collected delinquent taxes, preserved order at the polls, took in stray animals, and cared for jurors when court was in session. Until 1893 sheriffs were paid no salary, instead receiving fees for services rendered.

Elections and Electioneering

In the 1850s county residents seemed to have far more interest in local politics than in events at the territorial and national levels—not surprising at a time when news traveled slowly and many people resented the fact that they had no vote in Congress. Where local politics were concerned, coalitions that had formed before or during emigration had a profound effect on voting patterns. These coalitions included a group of abolitionists from Indiana who had settled on contiguous farms in the Beaverton area; a group of families from the South who lived in the vicinity of Hillsboro; and another group from the Old Northwest who resided in the same general area. (Bourke and DeBats, pp. 25–28)

Groups like these could have considerable influence—in part because in early-day Oregon, votes were cast *viva voce.* That is, instead of marking secret ballots, voters gathered at the polls on election day to declare their choices publicly, with speeches and loud group pronouncements of decisions to vote for certain candidates or support certain positions. As Paul Bourke and Donald DeBats have demonstrated in their fascinating book, *Washington County: Politics and Community in Antebellum America,* the practice of *viva voce* voting helped to create an unusually active, involved electorate.

The old Commercial Hotel at Second and Washington Streets in Hillsboro served as a gathering place when important events like elections brought people from the surrounding farms into town.

This brick Courthouse, built in 1873, replaced a two-story cedar structure that had been in use since 1852. The new County Jail sits behind the brick building.

The Courthouse steps were a favorite spot for local notables to be photographed. The first two men on the left are unidentified, but the others are (from left) E. C. Hughes, W. N. Barrett, J. W. Morgan, H. R. Ford, W. N. Pointer, Phineas M. Dennis, William Waggoner, and Rodolph Crandall. Ford and Dennis were deputy sheriffs, Crandall a county judge, and the others Hillsboro businessmen.

Courthouse Square in Hillsboro was the site of many community gatherings, including a gala banquet held in 1899 to pay tribute to the county's Spanish-American War veterans.

The care of paupers was also county business. This picture, probably taken at the turn of the century, is labeled "the old county poor farm."

Right:
Road building was overseen by county residents who acted as district road supervisors, but the work was done by those who owned nearby land. This photograph was taken in Mountaindale in the 1920s.

From the earliest days of settlement, civic involvement was a strong tradition in Washington County. William Merrick Brown, a pioneer of 1852, built the first jail and was deputy sheriff from 1866 to 1870. He also served as a school clerk, road supervisor, and justice of the peace.

A Forest Grove man loses a political bet and takes his punishment like a man. He was wheeled around the Congregational Church Square and then dumped in the muddy street.

In 1928 a new Courthouse was built in the neo-classical style that was popular in government buildings of the time. That Courthouse (pictured here circa 1960) is still in use today.

Runaway population growth in recent decades has led to expansions of county services and the construction of various facilities to accommodate new administrative offices. (Top) This modern Administrative Annex was erected in 1973.
(Left) In 1990 a state-of-the-art Public Services Building was constructed across First Avenue from the Courthouse Square.
(Public Services Building photo by Francisco J. Rangel)

Maintaining a tradition of volunteer citizen participation and public duty is the Sheriff's Mounted Posse (shown here circa 1950). Other volunteer groups that are active today include Search and Rescue Explorer Post No. 877, VITAL (Volunteer Initiative and Training Assisting Law Enforcement), and SALT (Seniors and Law Enforcement).

CHAPTER FOUR

CROSSROADS COMMUNITIES

While Hillsboro functioned as the county seat, other settlements, located at various crossroads, evolved as centers where farmers from the surrounding area could bring their produce to trade for supplies; pick up their mail; have their wagons repaired, their horses shod, and their plows sharpened; and take advantage of some professional services.

Glencoe

One such settlement was Glencoe, planned before 1850 by Charles McKay, a Red River settler from Scotland who settled in the area in 1842. As the crossroads settlement grew, it boasted several attractive homes, a blacksmith shop, store with post office, church, school, Knights of Pythias

Left:
Charles Walter was Washington County's last blacksmith. He arrived in Glencoe in 1890 and carried on his trade for some seventy years—long after the village had ceased to function as a cross-roads service and supply center.

Old Glencoe, one of the first settlements on the Tualatin Plains, was founded in the late 1840s by Charles McKay, a Red River settler. The remnants of the village lie just north of Highway 26 near North Plains.

lodge, drugstore, shoemaker, doctor, and barber. The village remained viable for about fifty years, but in the early 1900s a new railroad line was built less than a mile away and many Glencoe residents moved to be near the line. The new town they helped to established in 1910 was called North Plains.

Greenville

Glencoe's fate also awaited Greenville, which emerged in the 1870s on the donation land claim of Franklin Pierce, a pioneer of 1852. A supply center for those who lived between Buxton and Forest Grove, the crossroads town was located two miles south of present-day Banks. Greenville's early status as a village was signalled by the establishment of a post office in 1871. Three years later, Pierce opened a store, to be joined in 1877 by Jesse C. Moore, another pioneer of 1852.

(Above) Walter Hill Gatrell, his wife Henrietta, and their daughter Marian of Greenville take a Sunday drive. (Right) Leonard Van Lom of Centerville stops his buggy at the Centerville creamery. (Centerville photo courtesy of Florence Vanasche)

For many years, the town had a second store run by Dr. Marion H. Parker, who pulled teeth without benefit of pain killers and operated a saloon and dance hall in his building. In its heyday, Greenville also had a blacksmith shop, a willow basket factory, and a Knights of the Maccabees meeting hall. But at the turn of the century, as the town of Banks began to develop, Greenville's business—and several of its buildings—moved there to be near the railroad. (Fulton, 22–24)

Centerville

A third crossroads village, Centerville, was located between Hillsboro and Forest Grove, just north of where Cornelius was later established. The village grew up on the banks of Dairy Creek, so named (it is believed) because men from the

Greenville had two rival stores—one operated by Franklin Pierce and Jesse Moore, the other (shown here) by Dr. Marion Parker. Depending on which U.S. president was in office, the post office moved back and forth between the two stores.

Today, no trace of the village remains, but it once provided the services needed by farmers from miles around: a store, sawmill, gristmill, and blacksmith shop. Centerville also had a creamery, saloon, and warehouse for cargo shipped to market by steamboat. In a room at the warehouse, dances were held, and an Englishman, Sam Moon, trained young men from the area to box.

Hudson's Bay Company once pastured cows near it and made butter and cheese, which they took back over the Logie Trail to the company farm on Sauvie Island.

Neighbors gather for a barn raising at the Van Lom farm near Centerville. (Courtesy of Florence Vanasche)

At the turn of the century, much of Centerville's business moved to Cornelius to be near the rail line. The store on the left in this photo, however, moved circa one mile north to Schiefflin (the original spelling), another rail stop.

Henry Van Lom of Centerville delivers vegetables to Portland. (Courtesy of Florence Vanasche)

Centerville remained vital and active until some time after the turn of the century, when the town of Cornelius drew business away to its more advantageous location beside a rail line.

Bridgeport

At the other side of the county, the tiny village of Bridgeport grew up where the Boones Ferry-Portland Road crossed the Tualatin River. By 1876 it consisted of a general store operated by G. F. Orchards, a boarding house owned by Fannie Walker, a blacksmith shop operated by Billy Greenwood, and a saloon run by Joe Barnes. That village would later become Tualatin. (Martinazzi and Nyberg, p. 61)

West Tuality (Forest Grove)

On the West Tualatin Plains, a fifth crossroads community—West Tuality (now Forest Grove)—developed around a Congregational Church whose pastor was the unsuccessful missionary Harvey Clark. The first church on the Tualatin Plains had been John Smith Griffin's tiny congregation, which formed in 1842 on the East Plains but also served parishioners on the West Plains. Unfortunately, Griffin's rigid approach to religion soured a handful of his West Plains parishioners, and in 1845 they "dismissed" Griffin and called Harvey Clark to be their pastor. The new church's mission would be to serve Oregon Trail migrants, but its founders soon took on a much more ambitious task: the founding of an educational academy and—ultimately—a university.

Harvey Clark, first pastor of the Congregational Church in West Tuality, brought enlightened ideas about social issues to his work there. (Courtesy of the United Church of Christ, Forest Grove)

The first person to suggest starting a school was sixty-seven-year-old Tabitha Brown, who crossed the continent in 1846 at the age of sixty-six and met the Clarks in 1847. While staying at their home that winter, she discussed her concern for children whose parents had died on the Oregon Trail and told of her desire to minister to them. With Harvey Clark's encouragement and the tiny West Plains community's help, she was able to open a school the following year.

By the time she did, two missionary couples—Henry and Eliza Spalding and Myra and Cushing Eells—had arrived in the West Plains, nearly destitute and in need of work. They had been forced to close their missions east of the Cascades in the aftermath of the tragic Indian attack on the Whitman Mission and had been taken in by Harvey Clark, A. T. Smith, William Geiger, and other Congregationalists.

Mrs. Spalding apparently was hired to teach in Tabitha Brown's new orphan school that first year, while Tabitha cared for the children in a new log boarding house built by the men of the congregation. Her charges remembered fondly that she cooked for them with beef supplied by the church and vegetables from her own garden, took them on

Reverend Harvey Clark's log house was one of a handful in West Tuality (Forest Grove) when plans were laid to start an orphan school that would soon become Tualatin Academy and, later, Pacific University. The school opened in March 1848. (Pacific University Archives)

outings to gather wild strawberries, decorated the dining tables with bright calico, awakened them with song, and was their cheerful companion. Soon she was caring not only for children whose parents had died on the journey westward but for those whose fathers were gone to the California gold fields and for other local "scholars," regardless of their parents' ability to pay. Within months the school attracted the attention of Reverend George Atkinson, newly arrived representative of the

The school proved very popular, and Congregational Church members quickly erected this cabin as a boarding house for the students. Tabitha Brown was soon caring for over thirty children. Those parents who were able paid $1 a week for their youngster's room and board. (Pacific University Archives)

Tabitha Brown
(Pacific University Archives)

American Home Missionary Society, who encouraged Clark and others to expand the school into an academy that could provide the children of the new territory with a fine education.

On September 26, 1849, the territorial legislature granted Tualatin Academy an official charter, and in July 1850 settlers came for what Reverend Elkanah Walker described as "a grand gathering of all the region" to raise the framework of an academy building. The result of their efforts, the Old College Hall building that still stands on the Pacific University campus.

Difficult years ensued, when wrangling by the trustees and polarization within the community threatened to close the school. But the institution survived these ordeals, and many farmers in the region began to build fine houses in town so their families could live in proximity to Tualatin Academy. Today, many of these handsome homes,

ranging from the 1859 Classical Revival Thomas Hines house to the 1888 Queen Anne A. I. Macrum house, still stand on the tree-lined streets south of Forest Grove's downtown core.

From its earliest days, West Tuality was regarded as a cultural center where settlers' children could receive a quality education on the frontier. Its founders espoused the strictest religious motives, combined with some of the most advanced human rights theories of the day. As well-educated men and women from the Eastern seaboard, they maintained ties to a more sophisticated, godly world and were determined to recreate that world in their town. (Bourke and DeBats, p. 319) Elsewhere in the valley, their settlement was dubbed "Piety Hill" and their lofty goals were viewed with some amusement. But to a large degree the moral tone they set affected the entire county.

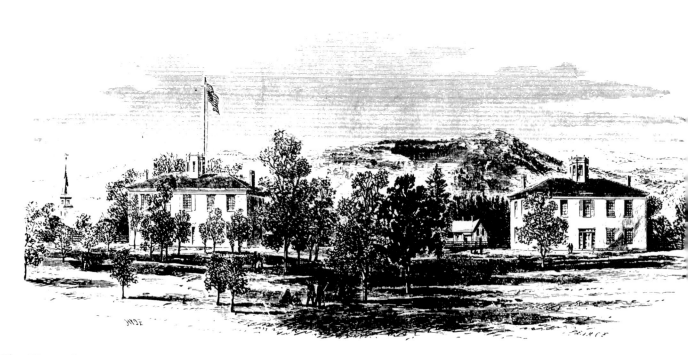

The Classical Revival building on the left, now known as Old College Hall, was built only two years after the orphan school opened. Its twin, Academy Hall, was built eighteen years later. (Pacific University Archives)

The Question of Schooling

The Reverend George Atkinson, the American Home Missionary Society official who had encouraged the establishment of Tualatin Academy on the West Plains, was also responsible for planning a system of public education in Oregon. That system was established by the legislature of the new territory on September 5, 1849 and soon began to replace private instruction provided by settlers in their homes.

The first elected superintendent of schools in Washington County was Congregational minister Horace Lyman, who began his work in 1850 and served until 1853. Lyman also founded the First Congregational Church and the first public school in Portland and was a minister and professor in Forest Grove.

During Lyman's tenure as Washington County superintendent, School District No. 1 was established, with David Lenox, Caleb Wilkins, and James W. Chambers as directors. In November 1851 they began to lay plans for building West Union School on the Holcomb land claim, and by mid-May 1852 the one-room structure was completed. The first teacher, Miss E. H. Lincoln, was paid $100 for teaching a twelve-week term. The second public school was Jackson School to the west.

In those early days, school was usually held in the summer when the weather was good but even so, attendance was spotty. The first districts were large, and some pupils had to come from as far as four or five miles away, although in later years, districts were often subdivided in response to petitions from parents.

Often, the first school in a district was built of logs on a timbered tract provided by a donation land claim holder. Desks, benches, and floors were usually crafted from split logs, while a fireplace might provide heat. Until the 1880s, teachers could be hired with a relatively small amount of formal preparation—an eighth grade education or a year or two at Tualatin Academy. A permit to teach required only a brief test until state exams were instituted.

The first public schoolhouse in Washington County was erected in 1852 at West Union.

Like this log school at Iowa Hill, many were built where trees were abundant and the building could be erected quickly. One teacher said, "The neighbors rolled up a small log house and put a mud chimney in it. It would have been a capital place to smoke meat in." His pupils went on to become the editor of a medical journal, a college president, a congressman, and a governor of Oregon.

Hillside School, pictured circa 1892, is one of several old rural schools in the county that still exist. The building was carefully preserved by Hillside residents Ruby and Lawrence Bamford.

Students at Arcade School on Pumpkin Ridge pose for their school picture in 1906.

Below:
In 1908 Cornelius had a sizable student body, housed in one of the county's largest and most attractive schools.

Students at Laurel Ridge had a
well-appointed classroom in 1914.
Their teacher, Charles Hanson,
was a talented photographer who
probably captured this scene.

Right:
Boys from Hanson's school prepare
for a game of baseball, while two
of the girls watch.

High schools were a late development, resisted vehemently by many residents, who considered them frivolous. This home economics class was probably photographed in Hillsboro.

An unidentified group of children from Hillsboro poses in a photographer's studio.

Laurelwood School, established nearly a century ago as a private Seventh-Day Adventist academy, is still going strong today.

Another parochial school, St. Mary's Institute, was founded in Beaverton in 1902. In the 1920s the Ku Klux Klan tried to close down all of Oregon's Catholic schools.

At the turn of the century, students gather in front of Marsh Hall on the Pacific University campus.

A classical education was one of the goals of those who founded Tualatin Academy and Pacific University. Here, a theater group presents an unidentified Greek drama—probably in the 1890s.

A float in a 1914 parade through downtown Forest Grove depicts the history of Pacific University in its sixty-fifth year.

CHAPTER FIVE

AN END TO ISOLATION

The isolation of the early settlers and the limited agricultural technology at their disposal dictated that their first years on the Tualatin Plains would be devoted mainly to subsistence farming. When word of the California gold strike reached Oregon in 1848, however, many men headed south to try their luck, and others realized that the California gold fields would provide a lucrative market for their crops.

Before this time, trade between Oregon and the outside world had been virtually nonexistent and no towns had claimed to have deepwater ports capable of accommodating cargo ships. Even if they had, there were no roads on which to haul farm products to market. However, with the

Left:
Canyon Road, initially a roughcut plank road, provided a way to get early Tualatin Valley crops to Portland, where they could be exported to gold miners in California. (OHS Neg. Orhi 20702)

discovery of gold, several settlements along the Willamette and Columbia Rivers vied to become shipping points for Tualatin Valley products.

A Plank Road

Despite the rival claims of places like Oregon City, Milwaukie, Linn City, Linnton, and St. Helens, Portland soon won the contest because it *did* have a year-round deepwater port and could boast easier, though rudimentary, access to the Tualatin Valley. That access was a muddy road that had just been opened along the canyon of Tanner Creek (today's Canyon Road).

Buoyed by dreams of capitalizing on the gold rush, residents of Portland and the Tualatin Plains decided to improve the road. Acting quickly, they formed the Portland and Valley Plank Road Company, received a charter from the territorial legislature, and managed to lay ten miles of planks west from Portland before funds ran out at the end of 1851. For Tualatin Valley farmers, the road barely sufficed, and calls to improve and complete it continued for several years. In the mid-1860s, a

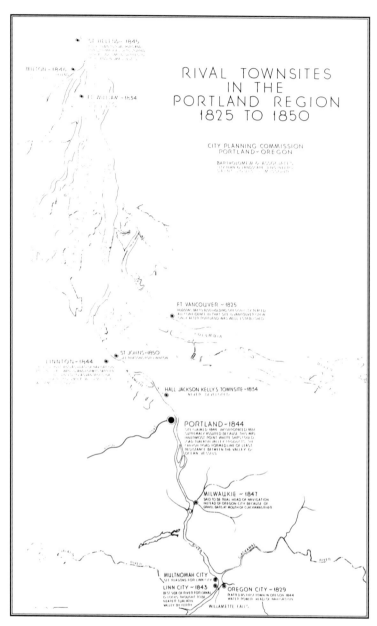

Above:

Buoyed by the California Gold Rush and the prospect of supplying the miners with food and building supplies, Portland's waterfront began to grow. Where ten years earlier only a few Indian lodges had stood, several frame buildings lined the town's "Front Street" in 1852.

rival road was opened that allowed farmers to reach Springville via Linnton, and *The Oregonian* was calling for renewed efforts to complete the plank road. A final attempt was made in 1872, but the idea died when railroads proved more effective.

Steamboats on the Tualatin River

In the meantime, schemes to transport goods on the Tualatin River achieved some measure of success, as proponents sought an alternative to muddy or dusty roads. In 1856 the legislature chartered the Tualatin River Transportation and Navigation Company to improve the Tualatin for navigation and to connect the Tualatin and Willamette Rivers. The company was formed by John Taylor, who also operated Taylor's Ferry and built Taylor's Ferry Road in the southeast part of the county. (Martinazzi and Nyberg, p. 48)

According to Edward O. Robbins, the company drew up plans to connect the Tualatin and Willamette Rivers—either directly by canal and locks or via Sucker Lake (now Lake Oswego). It also raised over half of the estimated $16,000 needed for the project. ("Steamboat on the Tualatin," p. 12) The *Hoosier* plied a portion of the river for a short time, but the project had to be abandoned due to financial problems. (Martinazzi and Nyberg, p. 49)

Another scheme, the Tualatin River Navigation Project, produced a "railroad" at the head of Sucker Lake over which horses could draw a wagonload of lumber in twenty to twenty-five minutes. Thus, logs from the Tualatin Valley could be brought to Oswego on the Tualatin River and on to Portland via the Willamette.

The Tualatin River was navigated as far as Hillsboro in 1867 and the side-wheeler *Yamhill* was placed in service until 1869, when the *Onward* began to operate. (Timmen, p. 90) The *Yamhill* had been on the lower part of the river since 1865, powered by the engine from the old *Hoosier*. (Martinazzi and Nyberg, p. 57)

An eyewitness, T. S. Wilkes, recalled in 1927 that the *Yamhill* eventually ran as far up the river as Solomon Emerick's donation land claim south of Cornelius (a site known as Emerick's Landing).

OFFICE OF THE
PORTLAND & VALLEY PLANK ROAD COMPANY.

Original Certificate of Stock.

No. 49

$200.-

This is to Certify, That *John S. Griffin* is the holder of *Two* shares of Capital Stock in the Portland and Valley Plank Road Company, at $100 per share. This stock only transferable by surrender of this Certificate, endorsed by the holder to the purchaser, which entitles the purchaser to a certificate in his own name. This stock not transferable after any installment is ordered, until the amount due is paid.

Dated, Portland, O.T. *ninth* day of *October* A.D. 1851

Two shares $ 200.-

paid 10 per cent. 20.-

due $ 180.-

Attest:

George Sherman

Secretary

L. C. Wirtz President.

Book 7

Entered on Record, the *ninth* day of *October* A.D. 1851.

Oregonian Print, Portland.

(Above) To ensure a passable road between the Tualatin Valley and the Portland docks, private citizens like John Smith Griffin bought stock in the Portland and Valley Plank Road Company. Although more money was raised in the Tualatin Valley, most of the improvements were made at the Portland end of the road. (Right) Private individuals also helped capitalize steamship ventures. Thomas Tongue was a prominent Hillsboro lawyer.

The boats were operated by Captain Joseph Kellogg, a pioneer boat-builder and steamboat operator, who co-founded the town of Milwaukie and platted the town of Oswego. (Robbins, p. 13)

A new canal between Sucker Lake and the Tualatin River was completed in 1871, but the Willamette River–Sucker Lake connection never became a reality. Eventually several factors—government indifference to the need for dredging, the coming of railroad service, long periods of low water, and gradually improved roads—led to the end of steamboating on the Tualatin. While it lasted, though, that mode of transportation created some happy memories. According to Fritz Timmen, passengers bound for Hillsboro would have *a pleasant boat ride on the steamer "Senator" from Portland to the mouth of Sucker Creek (now Oswego Creek) and an overnight stop at Shade's Hotel in Oswego. Next morning's trip on the "Minnehaha" to the head of the lake was enjoyable, if it wasn't raining.*

From lakehead to Colfax Landing [about two miles below present-day Farmington] on the Tualatin River was about a mile and three quarters by portage railroad. Travelers often traversed the distance afoot just to see if they could beat the engine. They won the contest often as not. At the landing the little stern-wheel steamer "Onward" waited for passengers and freight for flag landings or scheduled stops to Emerick's Landing, . . . (p. 89)

Steamships like the Oregon *provided an early means of linking towns along the Willamette River, the Columbia River, and the coasts of Oregon and California, but travel on the Tualatin River was longer in coming. In the 1860s, when steamships served Hillsboro, Centerville, and Forest Grove, the river became clogged with branches and silt during winter floods, while travel was often halted in the summer due to low water.*

Passengers on the *Onward* often picked blackberries on the shore while the boat navigated the river's sharp bends, and one story survives of an Indian who caught twenty-three fish while waiting for the boat to make its slow progress! For T. S. Wilkes, whom Timmen quotes, there was no boyhood thrill to equal "the column of steam and smoke curling up among the tree-tops as the Onward [sic] wound in and out of the bends between the Minter and the Jackson bridges." (Robbins, p. 13)

The First Rail Lines in the Tualatin Valley

While local entrepreneurs were intent on improving steamboat service in the region, larger forces were introducing a new form of transportation—the railroad—which would forever end the isolation of the West and Washington County. In 1866 Congress passed a law granting land for the construction of a line from Portland to San Francisco and containing a provision that the Oregon legislature name a local company to build the railroad through the state. Joseph Gaston won the grant for his Oregon Central Railroad and set about building on the west side of the Willamette River. His route would pass through the Wapato Lake area, where he established the town that now bears his name.

Gaston had barely begun his efforts to raise capital in Washington County and build the twenty miles of track required of the grantee, when a rival—the mighty Ben Holladay—arrived in Oregon. Armed with capital from his lucrative Pony Express, freight, shipping, and other interests, he quickly began agitating to have the grant transferred to a rival corporation, the Oregon and California Railroad. Holladay's machinations—and (he later confided to Gaston) $35,000 in political influence money—worked, and he was able to complete twenty miles of track by the Christmas Eve 1869 deadline.

In 1870 he acquired the westside line, and by December of the following year, train service was available to Hillsboro; a new town, Beaverton; and other stops along the line. However, residents of Hillsboro and Forest Grove balked at giving Holladay free land in exchange for building stations in their towns, so Holladay made sure to build the tracks some distance to the south. As a result, the town fathers had to devise ways to transport rail passengers into town.

Holladay also established the town of Cornelius, tried to have it named the county seat, and told local residents they must ship their wheat through the warehouse of Thomas Cornelius (a member of the railroad board of directors and the man for whom the town of Cornelius was named). In retaliation, local residents mounted new efforts to build a plank road and for a time hauled their wheat by wagon, a move that cost the railroad $4,000 in lost revenue. However, in the second half of the 1870s Hillsboro had its own station, as well as two new businesses related to agricultural export. One was the Hillsboro Mill, which produced oatmeal, graham flour, and cracked wheat; the other was a wheat warehouse at the Hillsboro depot. No longer was Hillsboro merely a site of county government. Now it was a shipping point for farm produce and lumber. (Matthews, p. 133–34)

Forest Grove also could afford to adopt a "take it or leave it" attitude towards the new railroad. By the time the trains arrived, Forest Grove had daily stagecoach service for mail and passengers, making it unnecessary to rely entirely on rail transport.

New Towns— Beaverton and Sherwood

Besides Cornelius, two new towns emerged as railway travel became a reality. The first was Beaverton, which was planned by local farmers when they heard that a line would go through their area. In talks with railway officials, they arranged to have a station built near their land and promised to build a store nearby. When the first train arrived in 1871, the farmers' newly platted "town" consisted only of a log store, built by George Betts, and the train depot. Nevertheless, the town backers realized that this new transportation link would be vital to their future welfare as farmers and businessmen. (Mapes, *Chakeipi*, p. 59)

Two rival steam railway builders vied to bring their new mode of transportation to Washington County. Ben Holladay (close left), a ruthless tycoon who had made his fortune in various transportation ventures, used $35,000 in political influence money to wrest the government grant for the project from Joseph Gaston (far left). Even after Gaston lost the grant to build a westside railway, he continued to promote it and was responsible for the station and town of Gaston being built on the line.

Chinese laborers were hired to clear brush, do some farm work, and help build rail lines in Washington County. (OHS Neg. 016075)

(Above) J. C. Smock, whose house is pictured here, operated a gristmill in southern Washington County before the coming of the transcontinental railroad offered him the opportunity to have a depot on his land in exchange for a right-of-way. The house still stands in Sherwood. (Upper Right) Smock's store was a going concern by 1885, when this photograph was taken.

A decade later, when the first transcontinental line was being planned, yet another town—Smockville (now Sherwood)—emerged in much the same way Beaverton had. Between 1883 and 1885, when the line of the Oregon and Transcontinental Railroad was being built, a local farmer and gristmill owner, J. C. Smock, provided a right-of-way in exchange for being able to have a depot on his land. He platted a nine-block townsite in 1889 and built a store and warehouse. By 1890 there were seven commercial buildings in the town, as well as a large brickyard that employed one hundred people and operated around the clock. The town also housed railroad workers. Before the brickyard closed in 1895, a victim of the Panic of 1893, one of its owners succeeded in getting the town's name changed to Sherwood, the name of his birthplace in Michigan.

Growth at a Modest Pace

For the most part, the towns of Washington County—even those along the new rail lines—grew at a modest pace until interurban electric trains, providing clean, quiet passenger service to Portland several times a day, began to run in 1908. Nevertheless, the old steam-powered trains provided a predictable source of transportation for passengers and goods, and isolation from other American states and territories became a thing of the past. As Hilmar B. Grondahl put it in a 1932 *Oregonian* article, "The railroads brought tangible contact with other people—mail, eastern newspapers, styles from New York and officials from Washington, D.C."

By 1890 the brickyard in Smockville employed one hundred people. Note that one worker (upper left in this photograph) is literally "lying down on the job."

Only with the advent of the clean, quiet "electrics" in the early 1900s did train travel in Washington County become wildly popular. When the first Oregon Electric car reached Second Avenue and Washington Street in Hillsboro on September 30, 1908, much of the populace turned out to celebrate its arrival. The old Commercial Hotel is on the right, City Hall on the left.

This Potter's Mill steam engine was used to transport railroad ties for the Oregon Electric, circa 1905.

In 1914, six years after the Oregon Electric initiated service in Washington County, the Southern Pacific's "Red Electrics" began to run commuter trains six times a day. Competition between the two lines was fierce, but both operated profitably.

Top:

Even tiny settlements like Dilley had their own stations on the Southern Pacific line, which ran from Portland to Corvallis. As a result, local farm families could dress up in their finest clothes and visit larger towns and cities any time they wished.

Top Right:

For rural areas, getting to market remained a difficult matter for decades after the main roads were improved. A horse-drawn wagon makes the trip from Cedar Mill to Portland over Cornell Road circa 1920.

Below:
An improvement program on Second Street in downtown Hillsboro, circa 1880, involved "planking" the street. In rainy Washington County, muddy roads and streets were a perpetual problem.

Boones Ferry Road was a vital link between Portland and the southern Tualatin Valley. Here, crushed rock from the John Nyberg rock quarry in the Tualatin area is being used to pave the road.

Left:
The old Scholls Bridge provided an easy
way to cross the Tualatin River. Before the bridge
was built in the late 1850s, the river could be
crossed here only by taking a ferry operated by
Peter Scholl.

Above:
Annual flooding of Dairy Creek caused endless
transportation problems for west-county residents.
South of Hillsboro this bridge, built in 1905
across Jackson Bottom, offered one solution.
Today, Jackson Bottom Wetlands Management
Area is a popular place to view birds and
other wildlife.

CHAPTER SIX

BUILDING A SOCIAL STRUCTURE

Long distances and poor roads may have once posed serious problems for Washington County farmers intent on getting their crops to market, but those same distances rarely kept county residents apart. In fact, from the earliest days of settlement, the desire to recreate the society left behind in the East regularly brought people together.

Religious Meetings

Many of those early gatherings had a religious purpose. An early settler on the West Tualatin Plains, Alvin T. Smith, frequently noted in his diary that he went to the East Plains six or more miles away to attend a prayer or temperance meeting in a fellow settler's house. In 1845 he helped found the West Plains Congregational Church,

Left:

John M. Brown, son of pioneer William Merrick Brown, poses as Uncle Sam circa 1897. Patriotic celebrations were one of many ways the people of Washington County built a society that mirrored the values they brought with them from the East.

West Union Baptist Church, built in 1853, still stands. It is the oldest Baptist Church west of the Rocky Mountains and has the oldest cemetery in Oregon.

and the following summer the church sponsored its first summer camp meeting—an eleven-day gathering. Soon, large camp meetings were held by other denominations, including the Methodist Episcopal denomination at what is now Beaverton. (Mapes, *Chakeipi,* p. 47)

Despite the difficulties of traveling to meetings, early churches expected good attendance. At West Union, where a group of Baptists founded the first Baptist Church west of the Rockies in 1844,

(Left) A Sunday School class (probably Congregational) poses circa 1867. Despite the number of children pictured, only fifteen families are represented: the Adams, Brown, Carstens, Cave, Dailey, Finney, Griffin, Humphreys, Morgan, Patterson, Reeves, Vite, Wehring, Wilett, and Williams families. (Below) The Hillsboro Christian Church Sunday School poses in 1888.

members who missed more than two church meetings in a row were required to provide an explanation. In all the early communities, religious meetings were held in people's homes or in the local school until churches could be built—usually with donated materials and labor. In the east end of the county, Ames Chapel was built in 1853 where Scholls Ferry Road and Hall Boulevard now meet. (Mapes, *Chakeipi*, p. 47) Many of these churches were "supplied" by itinerant preachers who might visit a different area each Sunday.

Fraternal Organizations

Somewhat in keeping with an interest in religion was an interest in fraternal organizations. Masonic lodges were formed in the 1850s in both Hillsboro and Forest Grove, and the Knights of Pythias built a hall in Glencoe. As other communities developed, several other fraternal organizations were established, including the Independent Order of Good Templars, the Maccabees, and the Rathbone Sisters.

In general, fraternal organizations were formed to reinforce morality and religion in their communities, although some had their political sides and some provided their members access to inexpensive

Among the early fraternal organizations in Hillsboro was the Independent Order of Good Templars, shown (top) in 1880.
In the 1850s the group met in the County Courthouse. Another group, the Woodsmen of the World, is pictured (bottom) circa 1910.

insurance. In connection with the Civil War, the clandestine Knights of the Golden Circle terrorized neighbors they believed were Northern sympathizers. And in the 1920s the Ku Klux Klan put on a campaign to eliminate parochial schools.

More Worldly Pleasures

While some of the earliest American settlers put religion and morality at the tops of their social agendas, the Rocky Mountain boys and Red River settlers on the North Plains enjoyed more worldly pleasures. A wedding in 1844 ended in a dance that so scandalized and disheartened Reverend Harvey Clark (the officiating minister), he considered returning to "the States." From 1845 to 1847, the Rocky Mountain boys held dances to which they invited the crew of the British ship *Modeste*, anchored off Fort Vancouver, and they themselves were invited to balls at Vancouver and Oregon City and to theatrical performances on board the ship. (Tobie, p. 135) The North Plains colony of former fur trappers also enjoyed gambling, which resulted in court cases being brought by their more straight-laced neighbors. (Tobie, pp. 206–27)

Fourth of July Celebrations

Fourth of July celebrations—a popular county tradition—began beneath "the Five Oaks" at the Rocky Mountain Retreat in 1845 but soon spread to other parts of the county. For several years the largest celebrations—complete with parades—were held alternately in Hillsboro and Forest Grove—but others took place at smaller settlements. One newspaper article by a correspondent from Wapato Lake (Gaston) boasted of a barbeque attended by "people enough to fill a table nearly 400 feet in length, if all had eaten at once," and a dance at which the young people "tripped the light fantastic toe, commencing at two o'clock in the p.m. and

A Goddess of Liberty Pageant became a central part of the Happy Days celebration. The young woman who was chosen for the honor rode on a special float and reigned over other festival events. This float held fifty girls who represented the states and territories, while a second float carried representatives of U.S. "insular possessions."

98

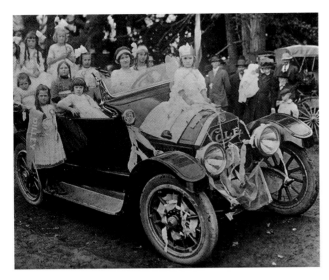

The town of Dilley had its own Goddess of Liberty on a car entered in a Fourth of July parade.

fighting it through on that line to 5 a.m. of July 5th."

Regardless of their location, Fourth of July celebrations in the county drew hordes of people from many miles away. And those in Hillsboro followed the pattern, established at the Five Oaks, of having everyone join in a parade. For many years, Hillsboro Fourth of July parades ended with lines of cars driven by anyone who felt inclined to join in.

In the final decades of the nineteenth century, local Fourth of July celebrations featured Civil War veterans of the Union cause (members of the Grand Army of the Republic) and veterans of the Mexican and Indian Wars, who set up encampments in town. One local historian remembers encampments at Naylor's Grove on the west edge of Forest Grove:

The soldiers' white tents were scattered all over the grove; each one had a camp fire in front of it and perhaps a table. At one side was the faithful old team and on the other side was a stack of feed. Near by would be two to a dozen old soldiers dressed in their blue uniforms decorated with badges of red, white and blue, swapping stories of army days. (Bamford, p. 33)

Families often camped alongside the veterans for the duration of the celebration, bringing their own food and enjoying the chance to share it with friends and neighbors.

Patriotic encampments lasted for several days and drew thousands of visitors. They featured morning and evening programs sponsored by a different town each day and showcasing that town's best entertainers and orators. In Hillsboro, Fourth of July parades that began downtown would wind their way to the campground and the day would end with fireworks. In later years, there were also rides—first powered by horses and later by steam. (Mooberry , pp. 113–22)

Other Social Encounters

Aside from community celebrations, much of the early socializing that brought people together occurred when they stopped at a crossroads community or took a trip to town, visited the local gristmill or sawmill or journeyed to Portland to sell wheat, flour, produce, or lumber. Perhaps the most frequent visiting occurred between neighbors, who often belonged to large extended families that had made the journey to Oregon as a group and had settled on adjacent land claims.

In the early days, settlers helped one another in numerous ways, from raising orphaned children to

Hillsboro's Tualatin Hotel, located on the north side of Main Street between Second and Third Avenues, was a favorite gathering place for East Plains farmers and their families "in town" for the day. The man conversing with the wagon driver is Reverend John Smith Griffin.

In 1911 the Tualatin Hotel was still going strong, thanks no doubt to the many signs that regulated the guests' behavior! The old landmark was torn down in 1919 when the Weil family bought the property and built their store on it.

Trips to the Oregon coast were occasions for neighbors to get together. Here, the J. W. Sewell and J. A. Imbrie families pose at their destination, Netarts-by-the-Sea, after a gruelling three-day trip over the Wilson River Road.

erecting homes and barns, harvesting one another's crops, and helping build roads. Later, as their farms prospered, several of these families made an annual summer trek to the Oregon coast, camping there and at several stops along the way, or camped together closer to home.

Brass Bands and Cultural Activities

The Hillsboro Band, formed in 1861, is shown here in 1895.

Central to both political rallies and community celebrations were brass bands, usually made up of town leaders. The first such group was the Hillsboro Brass Band, organized sometime before 1861. The band played for the county fair, marched in parades, gave concerts at various locations around the county, and stirred up patriotic fervor at political rallies. In November 1884 it even played for the big Democratic Rally in Portland.

To pay band expenses not covered by performance fees, the group raised money in a variety of ways—even forming a corporation that sold stock. Later, the band outfitted a room above the Hillsboro livery stable as an "Opera House" and rented it out for dances, high school graduations, political meetings, and shows by traveling performers. In addition, the band itself sponsored public dances at Halloween, Thanksgiving, and Washington's Birthday, complete with a special supper served at the Tualatin Hotel. (Mooberry)

Although the Hillsboro Brass Band (later called the Hillsboro Coronet Band and the Hillsboro Opera Company) was probably the first in the

county, others were formed in the coming years. By the turn of the century both Hillsboro and Forest Grove also had women's bands.

Those who weren't musically inclined often listened to lectures, took part in amateur dramas, or went to spelling bees, literary group meetings, or debates. In his history of the Hillside community, Lawrence Bamford recalled twice-monthly meetings of the Literary and Debating Society, with readings, recitations, and teams debating such topics as "Resolved the United States should help the Boers gain their freedom from Great Britain." He also recalled the annual Christmas program, weddings, coasting parties on snowy nights, threshing time, and "grubbing bees," when the women would provide food and the men would rid a field of stumps and brush. (pp. 25–27)

In Forest Grove, lectures were sometimes given by professors from Tualatin Academy and Pacific University. In the mid-1850s, when Thomas Condon spoke on natural history, one of his most faithful listeners was Mary Walker, whose many years as a missionary did nothing to lessen her

101

Top Left:
Amateur theatrical groups were popular in Washington County. Unfortunately, no details are available about this group, which probably was from Hillsboro.

Top Right:
Thomas Condon was a minister who served the West Tuality Plains Congregational Church in 1854–55. Later, he taught at the University of Oregon, returning to Forest Grove as a lecturer on the Chautauqua circuit. (OHS Neg. 55652)

fascination with the Congregational minister's Darwinian theories about how life forms developed. Condon, later known as the Father of Oregon Geology, discovered the fossil beds at John Day, in eastern Oregon.

The events that brought people together in Washington County's formative years may seem unsophisticated to us now, but they were the glue that held a new society together. As so often happens, however, friendships—formed and solidified over the years—had the effect of excluding newcomers.

Spelling bees remained popular from the earliest days of settlement until well into the twentieth century. This annual competition took place in Hillsboro on April 29, 1916.

A Fourth of July parade (circa 1911) in Beaverton marches past a saloon owned by Gus Rossi and a confectionery in the old Grange Hall. Beaverton had its own town band.

Members of the Grand Army of the Republic held their 1902 reunion in Cornelius. At these events, tents were pitched, gallons of coffee drunk, and (as one newspaper put it) stories told of "old times when war was h_ _ _ ."

Right:
The Opera House, run by the Hillsboro Band, was on the second story of the livery stable (right side of photo) and featured performances by both local and traveling acts.

It is tempting to think that this intriguing woman may have been one of the opera house performers.

Both Hillsboro and Forest Grove had women's bands that played at numerous public functions after the turn of the century. The Hillsboro women's band (pictured here) was under the direction of William J. Wall, who also led the men's band.

A Happy Days festival began to be part of Hillsboro's Fourth of July celebration in 1891. In 1909 the festival moved to Shute Park, a gift to the city from J. W. Shute, but by the 1950s more space was needed and in 1952 the fair moved to its present site across from the Hillsboro Airport.

Left:
Picnickers enjoy themselves at Shute Park. For many years, the Pavilion (in the background) was used as a roller rink and auditorium.

In Forest Grove, an annual Gay Nineties celebration involved a parade, a barbershop quartet competition, a ball, and other events. At the 1953 ball Audrey and Howard Tompkins (left) and Pearl Hughes and Marvin Emerson dance in full Victorian regalia.

The popularity of vintage cars like this 1909 Buick led the Forest Grove Rotary Club to sponsor an annual show, Councours d'Elegance, which draws huge crowds.

The Tualatin Country Club (in Tualatin), formed in 1913–14 by a group from Portland, soon became one of the West Coast's most challenging courses. (OHS Neg. 28373)

Competitive sports in Washington County have long enjoyed strong community support. Here, a group of neighbors has brought a team, wagon, and shovels to build a football field.

The Hillsboro football team circa 1897 included (bottom row, from left) Frank Stewart, E. Burk Tongue, John Bailey, and Adrian Merryman; (second row) Art Shute, Thomas H. Tongue Jr., John Moore, Charles Mitchell, John Gault, _____ Klineman, and John Connell; and (top row) J. Waggener, Gus Patterson, and Clyde Reeves.

Playing for the Sherwood White Sox baseball team in 1909 were (bottom row, left to right) Fred Parrott, Glen Baker, Ray Hinkle, Jack Parrott, and Chick Baker and (top row) J. Thornton, Arch Parrott, Charles Parrott, Van Northwick, and Oliver Todd. The man on the right (presumably the coach) is not identified.

The Banks girls basketball team poses in the early part of the twentieth century.

CHAPTER SEVEN

AGRICULTURE IN A LAND OF OPPORTUNITY

As Washington County "society" developed, farming remained the dominant occupation, agricultural products drove the economy, and the fertile land continued to attract new settlers. When the railroads reached the Pacific Northwest, the whole area became a magnet for recent European immigrants, who viewed the West as a land of opportunity. This attitude was carefully cultivated by railroad advertising and fueled by the Homestead Act of 1862, which provided 160 acres of free land to those willing to prove up on it. In the West, they found land to farm—something that only first-born sons could hope for in the old country.

Left:
Fruit growing, a proud Washington County tradition, began with orchards established for family use. Stock was supplied by pioneer nurseryman John R. Porter, whose nursery was located in the Verboort area.

The new immigrants began arriving in the 1870s, and many established distinctive ethnic communities throughout Washington County. German, Austrian, Russian, and Swiss immigrant families settled in such areas as Beaverton, Cedar Mill, Sherwood, Bethany, Phillips, Cornelius, Tigardville, Garden Home, the Laurel–Bald Peak area, and Kinton, leaving us place names like Kaiser, Susbauer Road, Schamberg Bridge, Germantown Road, and Helvetia.

Swiss and German Immigrants

One group of immigrants, the Siegenthaler Migration, consisted of several Swiss families who came to the county from the Midwest, in part to escape religious persecution there. Led by Samuel Siegenthaler, the migration included seventy-two people, among them Ulrich and Barbara Gerber and Johann Graf, who settled in the area now known as Bethany.

Bethany post office was established in 1878 in a store operated by Ulrich Gerber, a member of the Siegenthaler Migration. The store was also a stagecoach stop.

Swiss immigrant William Fuegy (lower left), had a blacksmith shop in the Phillips area. One of his neighbors was Tony Pogle, a Russian carpenter (lower right).

In 1880 another newcomer, William Fuegy, settled to the west of Bethany, where he farmed and ran a blacksmith shop that today houses the popular Rock Creek Tavern. The area, which became known as Phillips, is named for Phillip Pezoldt, a German. Other immigrants who settled in the county included the Kuehns, Stuckis, Wismers, Zimmermans, Kesteks, Lemkes, Hunzikers, Kuraltis, Brandts, and Schmidts, to name a few. In addition to other accomplishments, some of them founded churches that featured German-language services until well into the twentieth century. Among these churches were Bethany Presbyterian (1874), Bethany Baptist (1881), Bethany Methodist Episcopal (1895), and Reformierte Emmanuels Kirke, now Helvetia Community Church (1899).

Weeding onions for Italian growers was an arduous task that provided welcome summer jobs to local youngsters. This photo shows the Corrieri farm south of Second Avenue in Hillsboro.

Dutch Catholics Come to Verboort

Freedom of worship was the motive for another group migration—this time by Dutch immigrants who settled in the area that became known as Verboort. For their first year, the entire group lived in the big old house on the Henry Black donation land claim, but soon they were able to buy separate farms in the area. This Catholic settlement and the farming area that surrounds it still have a distinctly Dutch character, from the beds of tulips and daffodils that brighten rainy spring days to the huge sausage and sauerkraut feast the community puts on each November. In this part of the county, Dutch names like VanDehey, Vandervelden, and VanDyke fill nearly every rural mailbox and mark many of the roads.

Italian Families Specialize in Growing Onions

Some of the European immigrants joined their American counterparts in growing specialized crops. The first crop was onions, which early

After a fire destroyed its office and warehouse in 1905, the Oregon Nursery Company moved from Salem to a site northeast of Hillsboro and established the town of Orenco. The packing sheds at Orenco employed many Hungarian workers.

pioneer Augustus Fanno had bred to thrive in the area's damp climate and rich soil. In 1892 seven Italian families—the Cereghinos, Brasiscos, Patronis, Podestos, Baraaccos, Jacobis, and Reghettos—developed the "onion flats" between Tualatin and Sherwood. (Martinazzi and Nyberg, pp. 60, 92, and 122)

Orenco and Other Nurseries

The nursery business in Washington County was started by early settlers like John Porter but got impetus from a pair of German immigrant families—the Teufels and the Peterkorts—who established a nursery in the Cedar Mill area. In 1906 a site just northeast of Hillsboro became home to another large-scale nursery and a company town—Orenco. The name stood for the Oregon Nursery Company, which until then had been located in Salem. Once established in Washington County, the company imported several Hungarian families

Picking hops was a popular fall activity that offered opportunities to meet old friends, flirt with good-looking strangers, and in general throw care to the wind.

to help with the work. In just two years the town had a population of five hundred, a neat collection of homes, and a handsome house for Archibald McGill, the company's secretary-treasurer. Soon, packing sheds were built, along with a fire station, city hall, schoolhouse, newspaper, church, and stores, among other amenities. The nursery itself covered twelve hundred acres, planted with trees and shrubs. Its slow demise began just before the Great Depression, but during boom times it was a showplace for the county.

Other Specialty Crops

Outside Orenco, fruit orchards proved to be surprisingly profitable for their growers. Raised initially for home use, apples, pears, and peaches were later sold to canneries and prunes were sold to buyers, who would dry them for year-round use. The fruit trees on many farms were started from stock supplied by John Porter, an early nurseryman who is best known for bringing sequoia seeds back from California when he returned from the gold fields. His trees can still be seen in front of the County Courthouse in Hillsboro, at Visitation Catholic Church in Verboort, and in other county locations.

One crop that offered employment to entire families was hops, used in beer but also in yeast.

Hop growing continued to be an important crop until Prohibition. The season in Washington County was short but festive, drawing pickers from miles around and even Native Americans from the reservation at Grand Ronde. This was a time to meet old friends and enjoy what, for many, amounted to a vacation.

Nut orchards also proved to have economic value, initially for Ferdinand (Ferd) Groner of the Scholls area, but later for scores of other growers. Groner, the "Walnut King of Oregon," recognized the Tualatin Valley as an ideal environment for growing walnuts. He experimented with grafting walnuts, something Oregon farmers believed impossible, and eventually made walnut growing a profitable industry. Today, walnuts take a back seat to filberts, but the industry in general has remained strong. Depending on growing conditions, annual yields fluctuate between forty-nine hundred and nine thousand tons of nuts, many of which are packaged in gift boxes and sold at Christmastime.

Another crop—berries—began to be profitable in the 1920s, when several Japanese families moved to the county and began to produce commercially successful strawberry crops on a large scale. During the Second World War, tragedy struck many of these families, whose loyalty was questioned and who were sent away to internment camps. At that time, many families lost their farms, but some returned to their former homes once the war was over.

During those years, other farmers in the county faced a crisis because the men and women who usually picked their crops were either fighting over-

As migrant families began to settle in the county, Centro Cultural was built in Cornelius to provide needed services. Centro—the result of grassroots efforts by a few Hispanic families to provide a cultural center—celebrated its twenty-fifth anniversary in 1997. This photograph was taken at the fifteenth anniversary celebration. (Photo by Francisco J. Rangel)

seas or employed in wartime industries. To alleviate the problem, the federal government began the Bracero Program, which imported Mexican men to work in the fields. Even after the Bracero Program ended, many migrants from Mexico and the southwestern United States made the annual trek north to help with the harvests—this time bringing their wives and children.

Here, as elsewhere in the United States, conditions at the farm labor camps were often primitive and unsanitary, leading to federal and state laws that would improve the workers' lot. As the years passed, many migrant families settled in Washington County and gradually began to

Enedelia Hernandez once attended Echo Shaw School in Cornelius as the daughter of migrant workers. Today, she holds a law degree and is the school's principal. (Photo by Francisco J. Rangel)

This winery on David Hill Road northwest of Forest Grove was established by Adolf Reuter in 1883. The original home is now the tasting room of Laurel Ridge Winery.

be assimilated into the larger community—but not without triggering unfavorable reactions from some longtime residents.

In the postwar years, the strawberry harvests also provided summertime work for youngsters in the county, causing many a parent to stagger out of bed at 5:00 a.m. to pack lunches and get their kids moving in time to catch the "berry bus."

Wineries

Today, Washington County enjoys a reputation as a place where fine wines are produced. The first winery in the county, and one of the first in Oregon, was established circa 1883 by German immigrant Adolph Reuter northwest of Forest Grove. (At one time or another, before Prohibition forced their closure, that area—known as Wine Hill—had eight wineries.)

The county's modern wine industry began in 1965 when Charles Courey, a Californian, opened a winery on Wine Hill. When he sold the operation, it was renamed Reuter's Hill, after Adolph Reuter. In 1970 Ron Vuylsteke established Oak Knoll, south of Hillsboro, and three years later Bill Malkmus and Bill Fuller started Tualatin Vineyards northwest of Forest Grove. Other wineries in the county include Shafer Vineyard Cellars, northwest of Forest Grove; Montinore Vineyards, at the old Forbis estate in Dilley; and Cooper Mountain and Ponzi Vineyards near Scholls.

Hobby Farms and Horse Racing

During its formative years, Washington County was the site of several large "hobby" farms and race tracks: Spring Hill Farm south of Forest Grove, the James farm south of Cornelius, the John

Francis Forbis farm at Dilley (now the home of Montinore Vineyards), the Lloyd Frank estate in east county, and Hawthorne Farms and Thomas Tongue's ranch near Hillsboro.

One of the most prominent country estates, however, belonged to Simeon Reed, for whom Reed College and Reedville are named. Unlike some of his wealthy contemporaries, Reed was a serious farmer, who earned a reputation for improving agriculture in the county through the introduction of pure-bred cattle, sheep, and pigs and through experiments that proved the efficacy of crop rotation. Reed also raced horses at his farm, which lay just off the present-day Tualatin Valley Highway between 214th and 219th Avenues.

Beginning in the 1870s Simeon Reed, a wealthy Portland businessman, had a farm and racetrack in what is now Reedville. After the farm was abandoned, only a line of poplars along the Tualatin Valley Highway remained to mark the site. (OHS Negs. 42548 and 42779)

Harold Ray, owner of Hawthorne Farms, shows off one of his champion racehorses.

The Forbis Estate in Dilley once belonged to a gentleman farmer. Today it is home to Montinore Vineyards.

Pride of ownership is evident in the picture-perfect farm of Tom Ott, which stood on the eastern edge of Forest Grove.

Preparing homemade sausage for the annual sausage and sauerkraut dinner in Verboort has long been a community enterprise. The dinner in the little Dutch farming settlement draws thousands from the greater Portland area.

The Hunzikers, a Swiss family, farmed in Garden Home. According to one account, "it was not unusual . . . to hear Swiss men yodeling in the summer mornings." (Mapes, Traces of the Past, p. 142)

Oregon's first milk condenser was built in 1902 by Dr. J. P. Tamiesie in Hillsboro. Through good weather and bad, many farmers made daily trips over rough country roads to deliver their milk to his Oregon Condensed Milk Company.

The Condensed Milk Company at Carnation, on the southern edge of Forest Grove, entered this float in the Forest Grove Fourth of July parade in 1909, complete with a western Oregon touch—umbrellas!

Large dairies became profitable in the 1930s when new dams on the Columbia River made cheap electricity available and farmers could install milking machines, sterilization equipment, and cooling systems. The man in the photo is Arthur Ireland.

Hay baling operations like this were typical sights in the Tualatin Valley. This crew was helping a neighbor on a farm near Forest Grove, circa 1885.

Oats, once grown only as feed, became an important early crop in the county. Even in 1912–14, the period when this photograph was taken, old-fashioned horsepower was often used for harvests.

Henry Bishop Sr. rides a horse-drawn binder in Helvetia.

Eugene Dant (second man from the right) tries out his "new" threshing machine on the Jason Sewell farm near Reedville in 1882. Originally run by old-fashioned "horse power," the machine had been converted to steam. In addition to Dant, the men (from left to right) are Jason Sewell, John Sewell, Charles Hinton, Jerry Hinton, Sam Hinton, Sam Sorensen, Alex Allen, and John Parson.

Gustav Teufel, a German immigrant and pioneer nurseryman, poses in his truck—the first on the west side of Portland. His home and the original nursery were in Swedeville, near St. Vincent Hospital, but today Teufel Nursery, Inc., has large operations scattered throughout the county. (OHS Neg. 73347)

A proud crew, festooned with vines, poses in front of a large hop dryer. Once the hops were delivered to the dryer, the crew's work was done.

An early nursery, the Forest Grove Floral Company, was a harbinger of things to come. Today, wholesale and retail nurseries thrive in the county.

Left:
Beginning in the 1930s, Mark Lafky's farm in Tualatin specialized in irises and was one of the region's early flower-growing operations. Today, many other farmers grow bulbs, creating breathtaking displays of spring color along the highways and back roads of the county.

Members of the first Grange in Sherwood (above) and the Grange in Tigard, circa 1911 (below), gather in front of their respective meeting places. The Grange movement in Oregon began in the 1870s as a protest against low agricultural prices, high freight rates, and other inequities that affected farmers. Much of the organization's importance, however, lay in its meeting halls and social events, which helped to combat rural isolation. (Tigard photo courtesy of TAHPA)

The Washington County Fair

The first attempt to establish an agricultural society and a fair was made on June 10, 1854, when interested citizens from both ends of the county met at the Washington County Courthouse. After some false starts, aggravated apparently by politics, a second attempt to found a society occurred in July 1855. (Bourke and DeBats, p. 91)

The first Agricultural Society fair was held October 10, 1855, at Forest Grove and featured an address by T. J. Dryer, editor of *The Oregonian*, on soil improvement, an important topic in a locale where farmers planted wheat in the same soil year after year. Exhibits that year were spotty and consisted mostly of farm animals. A second fair, held October 2, 1856, featured some prizes for embroidery, needlework, and drawing. (Mooberry, *Argus* article, August 9, 1962)

This first Agricultural Society apparently died from lack of support, but another was organized February 9, 1861—this time with membership 135 strong and plans to own its own fairgrounds.

These plans took several years to reach fruition, with the result that fairs were held on the Courthouse grounds in Hillsboro, probably until 1869. By that time, the Agricultural Society had bought fifty acres just south of present-day Baseline and First Avenue for a fairgrounds.

When the land transfer was finalized, the Board of Directors arranged to erect a fence, twenty stables, a racetrack, and a grandstand. Running a fair was expensive, but rents from concessionaires, gate receipts, and rental of the track between fairs helped keep the operation viable. In 1882 the fairgrounds became home to many Fourth of July events as well as the fair. Then suddenly in February 1884, the Board voted to sell the grounds. (Mooberry, *Argus* article, August 16, 1962) The buyer, former Mayor Thomas Tongue, allowed horse racing to continue in connection with the fair for some years to come, but other events and displays moved back downtown to Main Street. From 1925 to 1951 the fair was held at Shute Park. In 1952 it was relocated to its present home across from the Hillsboro Airport.

Right:
A marching band and livestock judging on Main Street in Hillsboro were among the many activities that drew throngs of onlookers to the Washington County Fair in 1900. The fair began in 1855 in Forest Grove and was moved to Hillsboro in 1861.

A stallion parade in 1891 draws
entries from miles around and fills
the streets of downtown Hillsboro.

Right:
Produce at the 1909 County Fair
fills the benches and rafters of an
open-sided building on Main Street.

Preparing young people to carry on the county's agricultural tradition has involved organizations like the Future Farmers of America and competition for prizes at county and state fairs. This FFA group won the championship in 1947.

On September 3, 1948, during the County Fair, a log cabin built by Ernest Schaer was dedicated by William Hare (standing center) on behalf of the Native Sons and Daughters and the Washington County Historical Society. The woman standing in the doorway of the cabin is Ruth Gates, a granddaughter of mountain man Joseph Meek.

CHAPTER EIGHT

THE GROWTH OF TOWNS

The late 1800s brought growth to Washington County, especially to Forest Grove and Hillsboro. It was a time when new possibilities—electricity, the telephone, streetlighting, central water supplies, and sewage systems—made towns across the nation think in terms of expansion.

Forest Grove

During the 1870s Forest Grove acquired several new homes and businesses. By the end of the decade, ten stores, three hotels, and a meeting hall were clustered around the Congregational Church square. Although the town had been platted in the 1850s, when Harvey Clark donated land to

Left:
Brick buildings and sidewalks were but two of the improvements that Washington County towns underwent just before and after the turn of the century. The Woods and Caples store, built in Forest Grove in 1893, was a general merchandise store. Today it is on the National Register of Historic Places.

Tualatin Academy, legal incorporation didn't come until 1872. Once it did, many improvements followed, including provisions to control the sale of liquor, the firing of guns, the speed with which horses could be driven (six mph), the places they could go (anywhere but on the sidewalks), and the practice of letting sheep, pigs, and cows run loose. The town's Board of Trustees also prohibited anyone from cutting down or marring a tree within the town limits without permission from the street commissioner—a move that may be responsible for the town's sylvan appearance today.

Streetlighting began in 1880 with oil lamps, followed in 1888 by limited street arc lighting using excess power supplied by the Forest Grove Cannery Company and generated by E. W. Haines' hydro plant on Gales Creek. In that same year, another local businessman, Samuel Hughes, built the town's first switchboard and began telephone service for twelve customers, earning the distinction of having Oregon's first independent telephone system. During this decade, Forest Grove also developed limited water service, but home

(Above) The appearance of a hotel in the 1860s signalled a period of modest growth for Forest Grove, which was a stagecoach stop on the route between Portland and Yamhill. The hotel, affectionately known as "Mother Sloan's," stood for many years on the south side of Pacific Avenue. (Top Right) The Western Hotel on Pacific Avenue—probably built in the 1870s—was another popular gathering place in Forest Grove. Note the streetlamp on the corner.

lighting was slower to come. Meanwhile, E. W. Haines was supplying power to Cornelius, Gaston, and Dilley, and in 1890 Samuel Hughes began stringing telephone wires along the roads to Greenville, Cornelius, Vernonia, and other towns.

Eighteen ninety-four was a banner year for Forest Grove residents—a year when they passed a bond measure to create their own municipal water and light system, organized a volunteer hook and ladder company, and installed more telephones. For the next fifteen years, however, the water supply was used only for fire control and irrigation.

By the end of the century, Forest Grove had approximately thirteen hundred residents, forty businesses, fifteen miles of boardwalk, a new charter naming it a *city*, and a mayor/city council form of government. Within the next three years street-lighting was improved, the city undertook a beautification program, and a horse-drawn trolley was carrying passengers into town from the Southern Pacific stop at Carnation. The coming of the Southern Pacific and Oregon Electric commuter trains soon brought a flurry of growth that included six new additions to the city, a new elementary school, a city library, street paving, and an expanded downtown. Now Forest Grove was indeed a transportation center for west county farmers.

(Top) Modern improvements in Forest Grove included this power station at Carnation, which the city purchased in 1894 to operate its arc street lamps and to supply power to some residents. (Middle) With the advent of electricity, women gradually found more work outside the home—often as telephone operators. (Bottom) For a few years, Forest Grove had its own streetcar to ferry passengers into town from the railroad depot at Carnation. In this 1910 photograph, motorman Frank Bear is in front and attendant Floyd Loomis is on the rear step.

Hillsboro and Cornelius

In Hillsboro the 1870s were also a time of steady growth, with the addition of several wooden buildings—both homes and businesses that catered primarily to a family trade. (Matthews, p. 131) In 1876 the town received a charter from the state legislature and the Hillsboro Board of Trustees was established. Hillsboro started operating its own water and light system in 1892–93, providing the town with three fire hydrants and limited street-lighting, but modern sanitation service didn't come until 1911, when the city set up a sanitary sewer district and a storm drainage system. Meanwhile, local promoters began to advertise to prospective homebuyers, including Portlanders, who—the promotional rhetoric went—could now live in the country and commute to the city by rail in only fifty minutes.

In Cornelius, businesses grew up near a warehouse (right) belonging to Colonel T. R. Cornelius. The warehouse was the destination for long lines of wagons waiting to unload farm products, lumber, and other goods that would be shipped to market by rail.

This post office and general store served as a community center in the 1880s, when East Butte became Tigardville.

Cornelius, established in the early 1870s three miles west of Hillsboro, also grew. In 1893 the town was incorporated and began passing ordinances to control wandering cattle, regulate saloons, and institute various civic improvements. After the turn of the century a library, opera house, racetrack, and skating rink were added, but the coming of the automobile caused the town's importance as a railway shipping point to wane.

With the coming of the commuter trains, Tigardville began to grow up along present-day Main Street, and the town's name was changed to Tigard. In 1911 the east side of the street offered shoppers (from left) a dry goods store, grocery store, pool hall and barber shop, and plumbing shop. (Courtesy of TAHPA)

New Electric Railway Service Spurs Growth for Tigard and Beaverton

In 1908 several parts of the county, including Capitol Hill, Multnomah, Greenburg, Tigardville, Tualatin, Garden Home, Beaverton, Orenco, Hillsboro, and Forest Grove, were reached by new electric interurbans operated by the Oregon Electric Railway Company. The interurbans spurred the growth of Tigardville and Beaverton and fostered several garden tract developments— the first attempts in the county at real estate development based on mass transit. These one-to-five-acre plots with names like Fruitvale and Gardenville grew up along the interurban right-of-ways and were promoted as places where city workers could have small farms.

Near the southeast corner of the county, the tiny community of East Butte had been renamed Tigardville just before the new trains arrived, and the village center had been relocated beside the new rail line. From 1907 to 1910 several new

commercial buildings went up. By 1908 limited phone service was being provided and in 1911 power was being supplied by the Tualatin Valley Electric Company, which also supplied power to Sherwood and Tualatin. In 1916 the Tigard Lumber Company began operation and some new houses were built with lumber the company supplied. But the population remained just over three hundred for fifteen years, and incorporation didn't come until 1961—just before the town began its phenomenal growth as a major suburb.

The tiny rail stop of Beaverton (one store and a post office) grew in the decade or so after its founding to encompass five businesses, a school, a church, a hotel, and some fraternal organizations. By 1881 the town even had a forty-nine-acre addition, and in 1882 local residents formed a drainage district to finish draining the beaverdam swamps in the area. Incorporation came in 1894, despite fears that farmland would be lost as the town grew, and indeed five new additions followed in the next fifteen years. In 1912 a three-story high school building opened, and in 1914 a volunteer fire department was organized, with other civic improvements soon to follow at the loud insistence of the town's four hundred citizens.

Business in Beaverton grew up along the rail line. The town had its origin when the site was chosen for a depot and a renewed effort was made to drain the swamplands created by the area's many beaverdams.

(Left) In Beaverton's early days, the town's Main Street was a simple affair. (Below) Once the town began to grow, however, its downtown expanded rapidly.

News of a New Rail Line Creates North Plains and Banks

Another burst of growth for new towns in the Tualatin Valley occurred when a survey was conducted to run a new rail line to Tillamook on the Oregon coast. When word of the survey reached local residents of Glencoe and Greenville, they realized that the line would bypass their towns. As a result, many people moved their homes and businesses closer to the new rail stops, and the towns of North Plains and Banks were launched.

North Plains was platted in September 1910, had a depot by November 1, and five months later could boast a population of 150. The town soon had a grade school, a Knights of Pythias Hall, two churches, a weekly paper, and a bank. Several businesses also sprang up, including the Mays Brothers store, which was moved from Glencoe. After the first burst of activity, however, the town failed to grow appreciably.

In the next town to the west, the story was quite different. Banks grew up at *Wilkes*, on the old donation land claim of Peyton and Anna Wilkes, pioneers of 1845. In the two decades preceding the railroad survey, their land was being sold off to new settlers, who considered it good for dairy farming. Among them were the Schulmerich and Banks families. As the newcomers moved in, creameries were built, and as Greenville residents joined them a commercial center emerged. (Fulton, p. 26–27)

The new towns of North Plains and Banks were proud of their achievements. North Plains (top) soon boasted a hotel and a meat market and grocery, and the Washington County Bank in Banks (bottom) made an impressive appearance with its Greek Revival false front. The bank is pictured during World War I, when a highly successful Liberty bond drive was under way.

Some of these people—John Banks included—combined their agricultural pursuits with a spirit of entrepreneurship not often seen in county farmers. The Banks family had property in Yamhill County and part interest in Hillsboro's Climax flour mill. A neighbor, Montgomery "Gum" Turner, himself a railroad man, heard the railroad was coming and saw the chance to open a store that would supply the crews building the new line. When Gum's brother Ewell applied to have a post office in their store, the name *Turner* was rejected in favor of *Banks* and the town received its official name. (Fulton, pp. 27–30)

When the residents of Greenville decided to move to Banks, they took their homes and businesses with them. Between them, the Moore and Creps families moved three houses; and the blackmith shop, Maccabee Hall, and post office buildings were moved, too. In 1906 the town was platted and the railroad started service. Quickly other businesses were opened and some professional services began to be offered. (Fulton, pp. 32–44) Soon, additional railway development would lead to the creation of several timber towns to the west, and vast expanses of forestland would be opened to logging.

The longtime president of the "Bank of Banks" was William Lincoln Moore, shown here (circa 1913–14) on a Sunday drive with his wife Marian Pickering Moore, daughter Alice, and son Charles Windsor (at the wheel).

Banks was a tightknit community. Here, neighbors enjoy a sledding party on Banks Hill.

At the turn of the century, Forest Grove had become an attractive market town.

Fires were a serious problem for most communities. In 1910 this fire destroyed the wood-frame Academy Building (twin of Old College Hall) on the Pacific University campus. Another huge fire in July 1919 threatened most of the area in and around the downtown.

This street (present-day Twenty-first Avenue) was hard hit by the 1919 fire. The Congregational Church (left foreground) had been built in 1905 to replace the lovely old New England–style church that had stood at the center of Church Square.

In the decade between 1880 and 1890, Hillsboro doubled its population (to eight hundred) and had a commercial district with about thirty-five businesses, surrounded by areas of new homes and farms.

The Victorian era inspired the construction of several elegant homes in the county. These two were owned by (right) Dr. D. W. Ward and (below) county clerk J. W. Morgan. The Ward home stood on Pacific Avenue between Main and A Streets in Forest Grove, the Morgan home at Second and Baseline in Hillsboro.

Right:
Hillsboro's new water tower and electric plant went into operation in 1892–93, offering the town fire protection and some streetlighting.

Town leaders gather at the Sain Creek Reservoir circa 1912 to inspect Hillsboro's new water source. Standing are (from left) Emil J. Kuratli, Harry Bagley, Judge W. D. Smith, George Bagley, William Barrett, Art Shute, Bruce Wilkes, and Al Long. Squatting are W. W. Boscow and Bob Hartramph and at the top right is Bill Pittenger.

Dick Wiley's saloon was one of the establishments that earned Hillsboro its reputation as "Sin City," and indeed it was a lively place. According to one local legend, Wiley's pet goose frequently became inebriated and staggered down Second Street, to the great amusement of patrons and passersby. However, to give the townspeople their due, they initially challenged Wiley's application for a saloon license.

143

Riley Cave was another Hillsboro businessman, who ran a hardware store and served as justice of the peace. In this photo, a gaggle of children gathers to see a new wonder, the bicycle.

Keepers of the peace pose in front of the Hillsboro City Jail, with Police Chief James Barry standing in the center of the doorway.

Dr. C. B. Brown (right) in his second-floor office at Second and Main offered modern dental services in high style. The man in the chair is William DeWitt Smith, and behind him is Warren Dobbins. Note the single electric bulb that hangs over the chair and the canary in a cage. If the canary died, it was a sign that the gas used as an anesthetic had reached a dangerously high level.

An active volunteer fire brigade, Hook and Ladder Company No. 1, was formed in Hillsboro in 1880. Ten years later, the town built a new City Hall and Fire Department Building, shown in this photograph. In the early years, the firefighters themselves pulled or pushed the fire wagon and fought fires by passing buckets of water, filled at a nearby well. In 1893 a few fire hydrants were installed, and in 1914 horses began to be used to pull the fire wagon.

To serve Hillsboro's firefighters, a group of women formed an organization called the Hillsboro Coffee Club in 1894, later purchasing this house on Second Avenue next to the town water tower so farm women would have a place to freshen up when they were in town. The Coffee Club also provided hot coffee, cakes, and moral support to the firefighters and sometimes put on programs of music and oratory to entertain them. One goal was to keep the men out of local saloons.

Past presidents of the Coffee Club pose (probably in the 1940s). They include (front row, from left) Virginia Hamby, Ada Patterson, Hulda Connell, Grace Collins, and Irene Amacher; (second row) Martha Brownleewe, Georgia Smith, Lois Walworth, Alice Connell; (back row) Jenny Weatherred, Zola Morgan, Mrs. Fred Engeldinger, Jessie Sewell, Jane Hare, Emma McKinney, and two unidentified ladies. The Coffee Club disbanded in 1997 after providing years of wonderful service to the community.

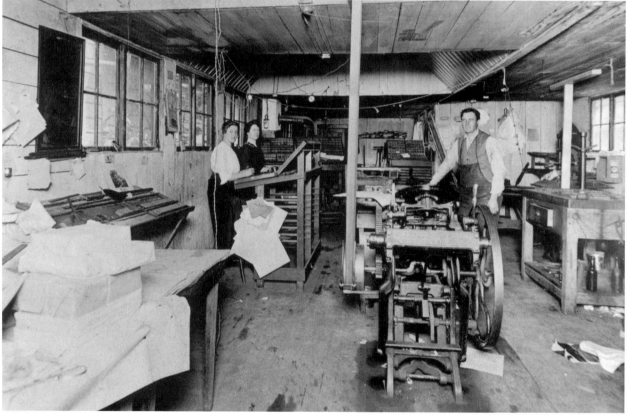

The Argus *has had a long history in Hillsboro. Here, Pearl Smith, Emma McKinney, and Carl Bunson get out all the news that's fit to print. In 1932 the* Argus *merged with another local paper—the* Independent.

The businessmen of Hillsboro posed circa 1893 for this group photo, taken beside the County Courthouse.

Left:

Good transportation, the development of industries, and the growth of towns went hand in hand. One important industry in Hillsboro during its early years of growth was North Pacific Clay Works, owned by James H. Sewell.

In 1908 limited phone service was offered in Tigard. (Above) Rose Scheckla is pictured at the first Tigard Phone Company office. (Top Right) The switchboard was an impressive affair for its day.

Germania Hall, built in Tigard in 1907, featured a restaurant, grocery store, dance hall, and rooms to rent. The building was owned by the Schamoni family.

Schubring and Biederman's grocery was a familiar stop on Tigard's Main Street from 1925 to 1950. The partners, August (Gus) Schubring (left) and Wilbur Biederman, also operated a feed and garden supply store. The man behind the counter is Art Biederman.

At the turn of the century, Cornelius developed its own business district and all the conveniences of a modern city.

Along the railroad in Cornelius were a pickle factory and warehouses.

In 1894 Wes Garrison demonstrated the first phonograph in Cornelius. On that solemn occasion, schoolchildren marched to the Hancock store to hear the strange-looking contraption play "Daddy Won't Buy Me a Bow Wow."

CHAPTER NINE

A RUSH TO THE WOODS

Where the Tualatin Plains meet the western foothills of the Coast Range, miles of rich timberland stretch nearly to the Pacific Ocean. When the county was young, that land held old-growth trees so gigantic they could be harvested only with great difficulty and moved only short distances by teams of oxen over skid roads. Even if the roads in the county had not been primitive and often impassable, horse-drawn wagons were much too small to handle the huge logs over long distances. Not until the advent of steam equipment and railroads could the immense economic potential of the woods in northwestern Washington County be profitably tapped.

Left:

As the rush to the woods began in the early 1900s, new towns and lumber camps dotted the landscape in the northwestern part of Washington County. Timber took advantage of its location on the Hillsboro-Tillamook line to build this restaurant, and a saloon and hotel (not pictured), that could serve both loggers and ocean-bound vacationers on the Tillamook Flyer.

The Rush Begins

In October 1905 the Pacific Railway and Navigation Company (PR&N), an Edward Harriman enterprise, was incorporated to build a rail line from Hillsboro to Tillamook on the Oregon coast, making the area attractive to both local operators and Eastern investors (who—after denuding many of the best forests in the eastern half of the United States—were looking for new logging sites). While the main PR&N line was being built through rugged mountain terrain, steep grades, and nearly impenetrable forests, logging companies began to build dozens of small spur lines, some only a few miles long. Soon the rush to the woods began, and logging camps and towns began to spring up along the PR&N tracks or wherever a private line could be built out to the main one. Author John Labbe of Beaverton was once quoted as saying that between 1910 and 1945 the county had between forty and fifty logging railroads. (*The Oregonian*, April 26, 1977)

Logging by Rail

During the early years of the twentieth century, names like Timber, Cochran, Buxton, Manning, Glenwood, and Cherry Grove gained prominence in the county. Some had been populated earlier, when a narrow-gauge railroad was being planned; some were transformed from sleepy hamlets into boomtowns; some sprang up anew. A few quickly became the railheads for several lines—eight at Timber, seven at Glenwood, five at Cochran. Together these logging sites drew large numbers of roughhewn men (once reported to make up half the county workforce), many of whom were based in Portland and moved from camp to camp whenever overcutting at an earlier

Early-day loggers relied on teams of oxen to pull large logs out of the forest over skid roads. The skids were logs, laid down on a dirt road and greased so that the loads were easier to pull.

site, a dispute with fellow loggers, or a case of itchy feet made a new job advisable. Many of these men were very young and of northern European extraction.

Work on and near the railroads, with their sharp curves and long, high trestles was unpredictable and dangerous. On private lines (needed only until an area was logged over), roadbeds were quickly laid, construction was haphazard, ties were seldom spiked down—even on a high trestle—and logs were merely rested on as many separate sets of

(Above) The difficulty of logging in heavily forested areas is depicted in this photo, taken of Lewis Carsten's operation near Manning. (Left) Carsten was one of Washington County's small logging company owners who also operated his own mill.

Frequent accidents on the PR&N earned the railroad the nickname "Punk Rotten & Nasty." This wreck occurred on November 8, 1910 near Timber.

wheels (trucks) as were deemed necessary to move them out to the main lines.

Camp Life

At the camps, accommodations were often primitive as men crowded together in small bunkhouses, slept on iron bunks with straw ticks, and battled armies of bedbugs. But one thing the men wouldn't tolerate was bad food. As former logger Francis Smith once explained, "If the grub wasn't just right, why, the guys refused to eat it, and they wouldn't work. That was one 'beef' that had to be straightened out right away. So, usually the cook got fired and they'd hire a new one and we'd try him." (Meyer, p. 55)

During the week, free time was often spent in reading, serious discussions of current issues, card playing, and an occasional baseball game. But on the weekends, the men cut loose at area dance halls. During the 1920s and 1930s, the dances at Shadyside (south of Forest Grove) and Balm Grove (Gales Creek) were the scenes of frequent brawls, fueled by the wares of local moonshiners. As Ralph Raines told Lloyd Carl Meyer, "I remember when I was a teenager, several of us would get together and speculate, 'where are we going to have the

Loggers take a lunch break at a boxcar that served as a camp kitchen.

biggest donnybrook tonight?'" One Saturday night at Shadyside, he remembered, a logger threw his combatant through a door with such force he landed in Scoggins Creek, which ran alongside the building. But by Monday, many of the altercations were forgotten by men who, after all, had to work side by side in the woods. (Meyer, pp. 54 and 57)

The End of an Era

The demise of logging as a major industry in Washington County can be traced to several events that peaked in the 1930s. Early sites were logged over and some timber outfits moved farther west out of the county. The Great Depression had far-reaching effects on lumber companies, mills, and financial backers. Labor unions began to seek improved working conditions nationally, and from a fairly early date organizing took place in the forests of Washington County, where many of the young loggers supported the concept of organizing themselves for better pay and working conditions. Initially the International Workers of the World (IWW) gained some adherents locally, followed by the American Federation of Labor (AFL) and the Congress of Industrial Organizations (CIO), but many loggers remained wary of leaders they suspected of being Communists.

The events that had the most potentially devastating effects, however, were the enormous forest fires in the area that became known as the Tillamook Burn (now officially renamed the Tillamook State Forest). Those fires occurred in 1933, 1939, 1945, and 1951 and ultimately destroyed about 355,000 acres and 13 billion board feet of lumber. However, through the efforts of local logging companies and a state forest rehabilitation program, the "Burn" was logged for salvage timber (what one lumberman called "charred gold"), yielding work for small outfits for many years. And in 1948, a $10.5 million bond measure was approved for a huge reforestation program that continued until 1973 and resulted in the planting of 73 million trees. During reforestation, families collected cones for seed, schools collected money, and thousands of school children, prisoners, and others planted Douglas fir seedlings. More than a half century later, much of the Burn is covered with new growth, and some limited logging has begun.

In the early days, the Tualatin River provided a means of transporting logs to mills. The men who handled this end of the operation were known as "river pigs."

Stimson Lumber Company dates to 1884 but got its start in Scoggins Valley in 1932. This photo shows the devastation wrought by fires in the Tillamook Burn.

During the first decades of the twentieth century, "high wheels" and horse teams handled the job of hauling single logs out of the forest. The wheels ranged from eight to twelve feet high.

With the invention of the steam "donkey" in the 1880s, logs could be dragged to a landing beside the railroad tracks and then loaded onto railway "trucks."

(Left) Much of the PR&N line had to be cut through steep canyons and sheer rock walls using modern equipment like this steam shovel. (Below) Surveyors and laborers work on the PR&N's Bridge No. 8.

A crew rests briefly at one of the stations on the newly completed PR&N line. Even after the Tillamook fire of 1933, the line was used in salvage operations.

Left:

Work on the rail lines built by logging companies was perilous. Here men stand atop huge logs balanced on "trucks" that are cabled together. Many a jerry-rigged load and homemade trestle like this collapsed, sending the men to their death. One accident that killed several people near Cochran occurred when cold weather caused the rails to contract and pull loose from the trestle. They had never been spiked down.

Fallers stand on a springboard to complete the undercut of a large tree, while teams of oxen wait to haul the fallen log away. Some trees were cut sixteen feet above the ground, leaving unsightly tall stumps.

The Timber sawmill (right center) was in full operation when this photograph was taken in 1912.

Buxton, at the foot of the Coast Range, is named for H. T. Buxton who settled there in 1884. For years, only the Buxton family and Dr. C. J. Mendenhall lived in "town," though a store, schoolhouse, and postmaster were later added to serve the surrounding area. By 1904, however, the town was booming and large-scale logging operations replaced the small sawmill that I. Z. Smith had built on the west fork of Dairy Creek, a half mile west, in 1890.

Three men pose by a bunkhouse at a lumber camp near Buxton.

Cherry Grove was established by August Lovegren in 1910 as a rural, Christian haven for the Swedish families who worked for his lumber company. The town soon had a depot, hotel, store, post office, building and hardware supply store, and school, as well as several houses—completely outfitted with utilities paid for by Lovegren. He also built his own railroad to haul freight and passengers from Cherry Grove to Patton, near Gaston.

Tables are set and a flunky (waiter) and cook stand ready for an onslaught of ravenous loggers. To avoid mutinies, only the best cooks were hired and in many early camps only men worked as flunkies. Later, women fought for the right to serve in the camps.

At the Gales Creek Logging Company, cooks and flunkies stand in front of neat bunkhouses.

Simpson's Saloon in Buxton was a popular gathering place for loggers, whose gruelling work in the woods gave them a powerful thirst by week's end.

John Burke, a worker at the Raines Lumber Company, finds out what happens to loggers when they misbehave. He has been strung up from the tongs of a log crane.

With the advent of the internal combustion engine, trucks
began to take over the job of hauling logs out of the woods.
Lucile Essner Stovall (far right, next to her husband Floyd)
was a log truck driver for Wolf and Johnson Logging Company
in the 1930s, covering the run from Snooseville to Vadis. Later,
she drove a school bus and a passenger bus.

Right:
Today, Stimson Lumber Company has a state-of-the-art
operation near Hagg Lake in Scoggins Valley.

CHAPTER TEN

WARTIMES AND HARD TIMES

In the midst of prosperity, America entered World War I. When President Wilson's call to duty came on March 25, 1917, young men from all over Washington County joined the Third Infantry of the Oregon National Guard, among other units, and were mobilized overnight. Some units were initially signed to guard railroad bridges, oil storage tanks, water supplies, irrigation canals, and other key locations in the county because it was feared that subversive groups would commit acts of sabotage. Other recruits were quickly trained and sent to Europe. (McKinney)

As the soldiers departed for their assignments, those at home took part in Liberty bond drives, knitted sox, sewed, made bandages, and in other ways tried to support the war effort. In Banks, the local newspaper issued a special call for men to build spruce airplanes to aid in the war effort. (Fulton, p. 71)

Left:
A high school training unit in Forest Grove prepares for service in World War I.

In expectation of war with Germany, recruiting for Company B of the Third Oregon Infantry took place at Hillsboro's Liberty Theatre on March 28 and 29, 1917—a week before America entered the war. The first recruits were four young men from the high school, who in turn recruited eighteen of their friends. From left are Sergeant Enoch Carlson, Guy Edson (seated), W. Verne McKinney, Clifton Bagley, Altha Russell, Vernon Olsen, and Glen Powers.

The Automobile Craze

As World War I began, Washington County was facing other challenges and opportunities—

The Forest Grove Garage (established in 1909 on Pacific Avenue) is surrounded by some of the town's earliest auto enthusiasts.

many related to the newest craze, the horseless carriage. As more and more people bought automobiles in the first decades of the new century, a statewide "Good Roads" movement got under way, and *Sunset Magazine* and other publications touted the joys of car touring. Soon, enterprising blacksmiths were scrambling to learn the intricacies of the internal combustion engine so they could convert their smithies to repair garages. Indeed a whole new industry grew up as automobile dealers became established and developed businesses, some of which are still going strong.

New Roads, New Challenges

The internal combustion engine triggered a frenzy of road building and so-called "strip" development that in the coming decades would change the landscape itself and alter the way commerce and government operated. As new highways were built and businesses sprang up along them, established town cores sometimes suffered. Both Tigard's and Sherwood's old business districts were bypassed when the new Capitol Highway was built in the 1920s, resulting in the need to relocate some businesses along the new highway. The same was true of Beaverton and Hillsboro when the Tualatin Valley Highway (Highway 8) went in a few years later. However, Hillsboro welcomed a new high-

In Hillsboro, lines of autos and electric railway cars compete for use of the street.

way, as did Banks when the Wolf Creek Highway (now the Sunset) was on the drawing board in the early 1930s. Leaders in both Hillsboro and Banks reasoned that the construction projects and new highways would bring jobs and prosperity to their communities.

The expansion that town governments envisioned, of course, required new skills, including long-range planning, fundraising, and cooperative regional planning for large-scale improvement projects. Increasingly, communities found themselves relying on state and federal dollars. For a populace that valued simplicity and self-sufficiency, such adjustments were sometimes hard to make.

In 1921 Banks incorporated after discussing the issue since 1912. Those who voted for incorporation were motivated by the desire for improved sidewalks and streets, as well as water, electricity, and sanitation. (Fulton, p. 73) In Hillsboro, the city manager form of government was adopted in 1924, a time when water and sewer problems, street paving, sidewalks, and zoning issues were also critical. In the aftermath of the war, both communities recognized the potential for growth and were preparing for it—in part by establishing a mechanism for paying for improvements through tax levies.

The Great Depression

When the Great Depression of the 1930s hit Washington County, hop growers and vineyard

William Ariss in Tigard was one of the Washington County blacksmiths who made a smooth transition to the automobile age, as these two photos of his shop indicate.

During the 1920s Beaverton became a moviemaking town when Premium Pictures of Portland bought a thirty-three-acre lot there and launched Beaverton Studios. Before the studio folded in 1928, it made twenty-six silent films featuring many Hollywood stars and using local residents as "extras." The cameraman was Gary Shields.

One of the films made by Beaverton Studios was Flames of Passion, *starring Pauline Curley.*

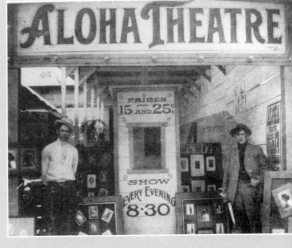

After the turn of the century, people fell in love with the movies, and theatres like the Aloha attracted eager crowds. By 1908 both Forest Grove and Hillsboro had movie theatres, run by Fred Watrous and Orange Phelps respectively.

169

owners were already suffering from the effects of Prohibition and many logging operations were halted—at least temporarily—by the Tillamook Burn. In towns the fallout from a depressed economy was also being felt, and the growth of some areas like Beaverton began to slow. At the same time, the railroads quit offering passenger service, creating a negative impact on the businesses that had depended on them. Outside Tigard, a hobo camp, or Hooverville, grew up beside the railroad tracks.

As the war years and the Depression took their toll, a populist movement that had swept the state reached Washington County, and in 1932 it voted Democratic. That vote came just after Washington County dairy farmers had gone on strike to protest milk prices—blocking roads and dumping milk to make their point. During the Roosevelt administration, however, the faltering economy got a boost as Works Progress Administration (WPA) and Civilian Conservation Corps (CCC) projects and federal funding put local residents to work on a variety of tasks, including construction of a new post office and sewage treatment plant, as well as improvements to Shute Park in Hillsboro; a new city library and concrete sidewalks in Beaverton; a new grade school to replace Lincoln School in Forest Grove; and a city sewer system and high school gymnasium, track, and football field in Banks.

WPA and CCC camps sprang up in rural areas, and some workers were housed in town, while churches and community groups took measures to help the unemployed. Meanwhile, salvage operations in the Tillamook Burn kept some logging companies afloat and provided work for west-county residents.

Another War

When the United States was drawn into World War II, the effects were felt in many ways. Young men were drafted, blackouts were ordered, rationing got underway, aircraft spotters and block wardens took up their duties, observation towers were established, Victory gardens were planted, and the community rallied to raise money for the war effort.

The first major impact of the war was the mobilization of the Oregon National Guard, whose Forty-first Infantry Division was sent to Australia and became one of the best divisions in

A bond rally during World War II fills Hillsboro's Main Street with supporters.

A paper drive also raised money for the war effort.

the Pacific. In the early months of 1942 the federal government made Oregon, Washington, and California military areas and ordered that everyone of Japanese ancestry be rounded up and sent to assembly centers prior to being relocated away from their communities. In Washington County, as elsewhere, Japanese-American families that had held citizenship and been respected members of their communities for decades had to suffer humiliation and loss of property and income. However, in a laudable show of friendship and compassion, many Anglo neighbors in the county cared for their Japanese-American friends' property until they could return to reclaim it.

On the county's farms, a loss of manpower to the military and to the Portland and Vancouver shipyards threatened the rural economy until the federal Bracero Program made workers from Mexico available to harvest the crops. As the shipyards drew workers away, many lived in the county and commuted to their jobs. At the same time, other shipyard workers were drawn to the county in search of places to live. The result in Forest Grove was a housing shortage that was alleviated only when temporary federal housing units were built in its parks. At war's end, the county was poised on the brink of a new era.

Newspaper carriers hold turkeys that they earned for outstanding sales. Three of them proudly wear hats provided by older brothers who served in the military.

Right:

In the anti-Japanese panic of World War II, the Iwasakis, a longtime Washington County farming family, were relocated to the Ontario-Nyssa area for the duration of the fighting. While they were gone, a neighbor, Ed Freudenthal, cared for their farm so that they would not lose it. The Iwasakis were able to return in 1945, but when they were removed from their home they didn't know if they would ever see it again.

War workers seeking housing created a shortage in Forest Grove that led to the installation of trailers in local parks. This aerial view shows Rogers Park.

In the post–World War II period, a group of women in Hillsboro demonstrates support for war hero General Dwight David Eisenhower.

CHAPTER ELEVEN

THE CHALLENGES OF SUCCESS

World War II marked the end of Washington County as a pastoral oasis on the outskirts of Portland. Shortly after the war was over, the Sunset Highway—begun in the 1930s—was completed along the route of the old Canyon Road and beyond, laying a ribbon of asphalt across the northern part of the Tualatin Valley and creating numerous opportunities for real-estate development. That development began north of Beaverton with the construction of a shopping center in Cedar Hills and a housing area, shopping center, and light industrial complex in Cedar Mill. Another extensive residential development, Oak Hills, was built north of the Sunset Highway at Cornell Road.

Left:

After Tektronix built its plant near the Sunset Highway and Murray Road in 1951, other electronics giants followed, drawn by the area's livability and affordability. Washington County is now known as the "Silicon Forest."

At the time, Beaverton itself was expanding to the south, but the new developments at Cedar Hills and Cedar Mill also forced expansion to the north. When the war began, Beaverton had a population of only 1,052; by 1960 the population was 5,937. (Dodds and Wollner, p. 6) In the years after 1960, Tigard's population also exploded, to be followed by Tualatin and, more recently, Sherwood. Now, cities that had touted their livability had their wish: people who worked in Portland were moving to the suburbs in large numbers.

A burgeoning population wasn't the whole story, however. The postwar economic recovery had also fostered a new electronics industry that would soon redefine the economy of the county. In 1951 the first high-tech company, Tektronix, moved just north of Beaverton after having outgrown its cramped southeast Portland quarters. Then in 1962 Electro Scientific Industries (ESI), buoyed by several defense and civilian contracts, bought one hundred acres near the junction of Murray Road and the Sunset Highway. There, the company built the Pacific Northwest's first science

Completion of the Sunset Highway just after World War II opened Washington County to rapid development, changing forever its character as a place dominated by rural pursuits. An aerial map graphically depicts the ambitious development plans that were triggered by the new highway. At the time the highway was built, Washington County had just over 40,000 people. In 1997 it had 376,000.

C.H. Project #2

Cedar Hills Project #1

100 Unit Manor Apts.

Proposed Trading Center

Sunset Highway completed - 1948

park, where it hoped to attract firms interested in research and development. Before the project was completed however, it encountered significant opposition from local residents, who feared pollution. (Dodds and Wollner, p. 18)

From the 1960s to the 1990s, as other industries moved to the county and the population soared, towns—especially those to the east and south—faced numerous issues related to their infrastructures. Roads needed to be widened and streets improved, police and fire capabilities beefed up, new areas annexed, and parking meters installed. In particular, the schools were feeling the strain of population growth, and bond measures were introduced to fund building and expansion programs. Those issues continued to demand attention as new high-tech firms like Floating Point Systems grew as spinoffs from their parent companies, and outside firms like Intel, Epson, and

Fujitsu moved to the area. Indeed, the county was constantly challenged by its own success, for in presenting itself as an appealing place to locate—a place of physical beauty with good schools, reasonable land prices, low construction costs, proximity to Portland, and (more recently) special tax breaks—it grew at breathtaking speed.

Of course, the high-tech industry only accounted for part of the area's rapid growth. The county also became an obvious place to locate large shopping centers and industrial parks—in part because ample parking could be provided nearby, in part because taxes in the county were lower than they were in Portland, in part because that city offered little room for large, new complexes. With industrial and retail expansion came the need for housing, and in recent years a residential building boom has covered large expanses of available land with new homes, apartments, and townhouses.

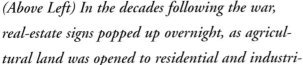

(Above Left) In the decades following the war, real-estate signs popped up overnight, as agricultural land was opened to residential and industrial development. Under Oregon's Land Use Act, passed in 1973, local governments devised comprehensive land-use plans designed to maintain a fair balance of land uses. (Above Right) As the area around Beaverton became sought after for housing, greenway areas and jogging paths were gradually developed. (Oregon Historical Society Neg. 73583)

Development has continued to be so rapid that city, county, and regional governments must struggle to keep up with it. No sooner are highways and roads widened and improved than they are choked with cars, inching their way to their destinations. No sooner are land-use planning regulations set than they must be reevaluated. No sooner are large, state-of-the-art schools built than they are overcrowded.

The character of the county has changed, too, as new residents whose roots lie elsewhere try to become part of the local decision-making apparatus, sometimes encountering resistance from old-timers. For their part, those longtime residents mourn the loss of the Washington County they once knew—a simpler place where you probably were related to your neighbors or at least had known them for many years.

Gone is the era of small towns, strung out along county roads and illuminated by a few streetlights. Yet the small town of yesterday offers a model of community fellowship for today's fast-paced world.

177

Even as the forces of change swept through Washington County, altering the landscape and way of life, people like Wess the Barber, shown here outside his "tonsorial" shop in Hillsboro, continued to do business as they had for years. Wess gave his last haircut in 1997.

In some ways, though, the county has come full circle. A new light-rail line from Portland to Hillsboro, may recreate the carefree commutes that passengers on the old interurban electrics experienced earlier in the century. As planners look for new solutions for overcrowding, one spot along the line—Orenco Station—is being planned as a village where attractive homes and shopping exist side by side and transportation is not by car but by rail. Indeed, many people now realize that the price of economic success—not just in Washington County but throughout the world—is a loss of community. As the people of the county look to the future, the challenge will be to keep alive the spirit of camaraderie and common purpose that existed when "this far-off sunset land" was young.

Just as early commuter trains tied a once sparsely populated Washington County to Portland, new Westside Light Rail service now promises to ease traffic congestion for the state's third-fastest-growing county. (Tri-Met photo by Tim Jewett)

Reser's Fine Foods, Inc., is one of Washington County's postwar success stories. When the Reser family started the business in 1950 in Cornelius, they produced and sold potato salads. Incorporation came in 1960 with Alvin L. Reser as president. Today the widely known company is headquartered in Beaverton, where it employs over one thousand people. In this early photo, Mildred Reser appears at the far right. Working beside her is Darrell Vandehey.

As the county attracted more and more new residents, modern home heating became a priority. Don Bretthauer started his heating oil company in 1953 at its present location on Washington Street in Hillsboro. With Don's son Andy as president, the company's operations have expanded to include cardlock gas.

Damerow Ford Company of Beaverton, with its prominent location on Canyon Road, began operation in 1953. In the years after World War II, many people were moving to the county and acquiring modern automobiles. Damerow emphasized customer service by offering both sales and service in its modern facility.

In response to a demand for air access, Hillsboro Airport got a modern control tower in 1965. The airport, now part of the Port of Portland, is especially useful to high-tech firms with business in the San Francisco Bay area.

In 1969 US National Bank's Hillsboro Branch was doubled in size to better serve the community. Its expansion mirrored the growth of population and industry in the area.

Henry Hagg Lake in Scoggins Valley is a large manmade lake that occupies former farmland. The lake, named for a well-known county resident, was created in the 1970s to provide irrigation, recreation, and flood control.

In recent years, Washington County has continued to be attractive to large companies like Nike, in part because of its livability and its proximity to outdoor recreation areas. Nike, whose athletic shoes and clothing are worn by people around the world, has its worldwide headquarters in Beaverton. (Photo by Francisco J. Rangel)

Where wheat fields once stretched as far as the eye can see, greenhouses like those at Iwasaki Brothers, Inc., on Minter Bridge Road, now line many rural county roads. These large nurseries offer year-round work to men and women who were once seasonal laborers. (Photo by Francisco J. Rangel)

*Intel, the largest industrial employer in Oregon, is adding
on to its research and development facility at Ronler Acres,
one of six campuses in Washington County. Its liberal bonuses
and stock plans have fueled the local economy, contributed to
real-estate development, and benefited hundreds of suppliers.
(Photo by Francisco J. Rangel)*

BIBLIOGRAPHY

Author's Note: The following sources are directly cited in *This Far-Off Land*. In addition, I consulted numerous community histories, manuscripts, newspaper clippings, and other resources in the collections of the Washington County Museum, as well as a number of books on Oregon history.

Abdill, George B. "Pacific Railway & Navigation Company." Washington County Museum Vertical Files.

Bamford, Lawrence E. "Hillside History," *Land of Tuality*, vol. 3. Hillsboro: Washington County Historical Society, 1975.

Beckham, Stephen Dow. *The Indians of Western Oregon: This Land Was Theirs*. Coos Bay, Ore.: Arago Books, 1977.

Benson, Robert. "The Glittering Plain," *Land of Tuality*, vol. 1. Hillsboro: Washington County Historical Society, 1975.

Bourke, Paul, and Donald DeBats. *Washington County: Politics and Community in Antebellum America*. Baltimore: The Johns Hopkins University Press, 1995.

Brody, Linda S., and Nancy A. Olson. *Cedar Mill History*. Portland: Brody and Olson, 1978.

Buan, Carolyn M. *A Changing Mission: The Story of a Pioneer Church*. Forest Grove, Ore.: The United Church of Christ (Congregational), 1995.

This 1900 photo shows Jim Lincoln Loving's blacksmith shop in Gales Creek. To the left are Ivers Jacobsen's Shoe Shop and the Berry and Dallas prune dryer. Mr. Loving stands in the blacksmith shop doorway.

Burnett, Peter H. "Recollections of an Old Pioneer," Oregon Historical Quarterly 5 (1904): 151–198.

Culp, Edwin D. *Early Oregon Days*. Caldwell: The Caxton Printer, Ltd., 1987.

Dodds, Gordon B. *Oregon: A History*. New York: W. W. Norton & Company, Inc., 1977.

Dodds, Gordon B., and Craig Wollner. *The Silicon Forest: High Tech in the Portland Area, 1945–1986*. Portland: Oregon Historical Society Press, 1990.

Fulton, Ann. *Banks: A Darn Good Little Town*. Banks, Ore.: Ann Fulton, 1995.

Gordon, Sarah H. *Passage to Union: How the Railroads Transformed American Life, 1829–1929*. Chicago: Ivan R. Dee, 1996.

Hesse, Margaret Putnam. *Scholls Ferry Tales*. Medford: Webb Research Group-Publishers for Groner Women's Club, 1994.

Jensen, Oliver. *The American Heritage History of Railroads in America*. New York: American Heritage Publishing Co., Inc., 1975.

Mackey, Harold. *The Kalapuyans: A Sourcebook on the Indians of the Willamette Valley*. Salem, Ore.: Mission Mill Museum Association, Inc., 1974.

Mapes, Virginia. *Chakeipi: The Place of the Beaver*. Beaverton, Ore.: City of Beaverton, 1993.

_____. *Garden Home: The Way It Was*. Beaverton, Ore.: Beaverton School District 48, 1980.

Martinazzi, Loyce, and Karen Lafky Nygaard, *Tualatin: From the Beginning*. Tualatin: Tualatin Historical Society, 1994.

Matthews, Richard P. "Limited Horizons on the Oregon Frontier: East Tualatin Plains and the Town of Hillsboro, Washington County, 1840–1890." Master's thesis, Portland State University, 1988.

McKinney, W. Verne. Personal Papers, MSS 49, Washington County Museum.

Meyer, Lloyd Carl. "History of Logging in Washington County: From the Frontier to the Future," *Land of Tuality*, vol. 3, 1978.

Minor, Rick et al. *Cultural Resource Overview of BLM Lands in Northwestern Oregon: Archaeology, Ethnography, History*. University of Oregon Anthropological Papers No. 20, 1980.

Mooberry, Lester. *The Argus,* August 9, 1962.

_____. *The Argus,* August 16, 1962.

O'Donnell, Terence. *That Balance So Rare: The Story of Oregon*. Portland: Oregon Historical Society Press, 1988.

Richert-Boe, Paul. "Timber Was Hub of 8 Railroads," *The Oregonian*, April 26, 1977.

Robbins, Edward O. "Railroad Transportation," *Land of Tuality*, vol. 2. Hillsboro: Washington County Historical Society, 1976.

_____. "Steamboat on the Tualatin," *Land of Tuality*, vol. 2. Hillsboro: Washington County Historical Society, 1976.

Timmen, Fritz. *Blow for the Landing*. Caldwell, Idaho: The Caxton Printers, Ltd., 1973.

Tobie, Harvey Elmer. *No Man Like Joe: The Life and Times of Joseph L. Meek*. Portland: Binford and Mort for the Oregon Historical Society, 1949.

Victor, Frances Fuller. *The River of the West: The Adventures of Joe Meek*. Missoula: Mountain Press Publishing Company, 1985.

Zenk, Henry. "Contributions to Tualatin Ethnography: Subsistence and Ethnobiology." Master's thesis, Portland State University, 1976.

INDEX

Italic numbers indicate photo or photo caption.

ABOUT THE AUTHOR

(Photo by Francisco J. Rangel)

Carolyn Buan is a professional writer who owns Writing and Editing Services in Portland. During the past thirteen years, she has taken on assignments as diverse as developing a driving tour brochure of historic sites in Washington County, writing exhibit text for the Oregon Zoo, editing and producing books, editing a small magazine, and writing marketing materials for a curriculum products software company. She is the author of *A Changing Mission: The Story of a Pioneer Church*, a sesquicentennial history of the United Church of Christ in Forest Grove, and editor of *The First Duty: A History of the U.S. District Court for Oregon*.

From 1972 to 1985, before starting her business and moving to Portland, she and her two children lived in Forest Grove, where she served on the Forest Grove Historic Landmarks Board—for a time as its chairman. During her years in the county, she also joined the board of the Washington County Historical Society and served as its program chair and newsletter editor. Those associations whetted her appetite for learning more about the history of the county.

Buan grew up in Anchorage, Alaska, which she still considers to be "God's country." After graduating from Anchorage High School, she studied drama at the University of Southern California and earned a bachelor's degree in English and a secondary teaching certificate from Lewis and Clark College in Portland, Oregon. After receiving a master's degree in English from the University of Washington, she returned to Anchorage, where she taught for three years at East Anchorage High School, directed plays, and helped establish a high school drama festival. Later, her travels took her to Norway, where she married, began raising a family, and taught English conversation classes at the teachers' college in Trondheim. Before starting her business, she spent four years as an editor-writer with the Northwest Regional Educational Laboratory in Portland and ten years as associate director of the Oregon Council for the Humanities.